POETRY FROM CRESCENT MOON

I0108834

William Shakespeare: *Complete Poetry*
edited and introduced by Mark Tuley

Edmund Spenser: *Heavenly Love: Selected Poems*
selected and introduced by Teresa Page

Robert Herrick: *Delight In Disorder: Selected Poems*
edited and introduced by M.K. Pace

Sir Thomas Wyatt: *Love For Love: Selected Poems*
selected and introduced by Louise Cooper

John Donne: *Air and Angels: Selected Poems*
selected and introduced by A.H. Ninham

D.H. Lawrence: *Being Alive: Selected Poems*
edited with an introduction by Margaret Elvy

D.H. Lawrence: Symbolic Landscapes
by Jane Foster

D.H. Lawrence: Infinite Sensual Violence
by M.K. Pace

Percy Bysshe Shelley: *Paradise of Golden Lights: Selected Poems*
selected and introduced by Charlotte Greene

Thomas Hardy: *Her Haunting Ground: Selected Poems*
edited, with an introduction by A.H. Ninham

Sexing Hardy: Thomas Hardy and Feminism
by Margaret Elvy

Emily Bronte: *Darkness and Glory: Selected Poems*
selected and introduced by Miriam Chalk

John Keats: *Bright Star: Selected Poems*
edited with an introduction by Miriam Chalk

Henry Vaughan: *A Great Ring of Pure and Endless Light: Selected Poems*
selected and introduced by A.H. Ninham

The Crescent Moon Book of Love Poetry
edited by Louise Cooper

The Crescent Moon Book of Mystical Poetry in English
edited by Carol Appleby

The Crescent Moon Book of Nature Poetry From Langland to Lawrence
edited by Margaret Elvy

The Crescent Moon Book of Metaphysical Poetry
edited and introduced by Charlotte Greene

The Crescent Moon Book of Elizabethan Love Poetry
edited and introduced by Carol Appleby

Peter Redgrove: Here Comes the Flood
by Jeremy Mark Robinson

Sex-Magic-Poetry-Cornwall: A Flood of Poems
by Peter Redgrove, edited with an essay by Jeremy Mark Robinson

Brigitte's Blue Heart
by Jeremy Reed

Claudia Schiffer's Red Shoes
by Jeremy Reed

By-Blows: Uncollected Poems
by D.J. Enright

Dante: *Selections From the Vita Nuova*
translated by Thomas Okey

Arthur Rimbaud: *Selected Poems*
edited and translated by Andrew Jary

Arthur Rimbaud: *A Season in Hell*
edited and translated by Andrew Jary

Friedrich Hölderlin: *Hölderlin's Songs of Light: Selected Poems*
translated by Michael Hamburger

Rainer Maria Rilke: *Dance the Orange:* Selected Poems
translated by Michael Hamburger

German Romantic Poetry: Goethe, Novalis, Heine, Hölderlin
by Carol Appleby

Arseny Tarkovsky: *Life, Life: Selected Poems*
translated by Virginia Rounding

Emily Dickinson: *Wild Nights: Selected Poems*
selected and introduced by Miriam Chalk

The Crescent Moon Book of Romantic Poetry

The Crescent Moon Book
of Romantic Poetry

Edited by L.M. Poole

CRESCENT MOON

CRESCENT MOON PUBLISHING
P.O. Box 1312, Maidstone
Kent, ME14 5XU
Great Britain
www.crmoon.com

First published 1996. Second edition 2008. Third edition 2016.
Introduction © L.M. Poole, 1996, 2008, 2016.

Printed and bound in the U.S.A.
Set in Garamond Book 10 on 14pt.
Designed by Radiance Graphics.

The right of L.M. Poole to be identified as the editor of this book has been asserted generally in accordance with sections 77 and 78 of the Copyright, Designs and Patents Act 1988.

British Library Cataloguing in Publication data

The Crescent Moon Book of Romantic Poetry (British Poets Series)
I. Title II. Poole, L.M.
III. Series
821.3

ISBN-13 978186171366
ISBN-13 9781861715296

Contents

William Cowper   To the Nightingale   11
Charlotte Smith   Sonnet: To the South Down   13
                          from Beachy Head   14
Ann Yearsley   Anarchy   15
William Blake   Night   16
                          Song   18
                          Hear the Voice   19
                          Mad Song   20
                          Songs of Innocence   21
                          To the Evening Star   22
Mary Robinson   Sonnet: To Liberty   23
                          from To the Poet Coleridge   24
                          Stanzas Written After Successive Nights of
                          Melancholy Dream   25
Helen Maria Williams   Sonnet: To the Torrid Zone   28
Barbara Hoole   Sonnet   29
William Wordsworth   from Lines   30
                          from Ode: Intimations of Immortality   31
                          from *Lucy*   34
                          "I Wandered Lonely as a Cloud"   35
                          Evening On Calais Beach   36
                          Perfect Woman   37
Dororthy Wordsworth   Floating Island at Hawkshead   38
Samuel Taylor Coleridge
                          This Lime-Tree Bower My Prison   40
                          from Dejection   43
                          The Nightingale   46
                          Frost At Midnight   50
                          Fears In Solitude   53
                          The AEolian Harp   61
Lord Byron   from *Childe Harold's Pilgrimage*   64
                          "She Walks in Beauty"   67

	"When We Two Parted" 68
	Darkness 70
	Prometheus 73
	My Soul Is Dark 75
Percy Bysshe Shelley	The Cloud 76
	Song 79
	from *Adonais* 82
	A Lament 84
	Ozymandias 85
	Mutability 86
	Song of Prosperine 87
	Stanzas Written In Dejection
	Near Naples 88
	To Night 90
Felicia Dorothea Hemans	
	The Rock of Cader Idris 92
Emma Roberts	Night on the Ganges 94
John Clare	A Spring Morning 96
	Love's Story 97
	To Mary 98
John Keats	Ode to Melancholy 99
	"Bright star" 101
	La Belle Dame Sans Merci 102
	Ode To a Nightingale 105
	To Solitude 109
	The Eve of St Agnes 110
Elizabeth Barret Browning	
	from *Sonnets From the Portuguese* 125
Mary Wollstonecraft Shelley	
	Stanzas 127
Edgar Allan Poe	A Dream 128
	The Bells 129
Charlotte Brontë	"What does she dream of" 133
Emily Brontë	"That wind" 134
	Loud with the wind was roaring 135
	High waving heather 138
	Stars 139

Mild the Mist   141

Gallery of Poets   142
A Note on Romantic Poetry   155
Notes   160
Bibliography   161

WILLIAM COWPER
(1731-1800)

To the Nightingale

which the author heard sing on New Year's Day, 1792

Whence is it, that amazed I hear
    From yonder wither'd spray,
This foremost morn of all the year,
    The melody of May?

And why, since thousands would be proud
    Of such a favour shown,
Am I selected from the crowd,
    To witness it alone?

Sing'st thou, sweet Philomel, to me,
    For that I also long
Have practis'd in the groves like these,
    Thou not like thee in song?

Or sing'st thou rather under force
    Of some divine command,
Commission'd to presage a course
    Of happier days at hand?

Thrice welcome then! for many a long
    And joyless year have I,
As thou today, put forth my song
    Beneath a wintry sky.

But thee no wintry skies can harm,
    Who only need'st to sing,
To make ev'n January charm,
    And ev'ry season Spring.

CHARLOTTE SMITH
(1749-1806)

Sonnet: To the South Downs

Ah, hills beloved! - where once, an happy child,
    Your beechen shades, 'your turf, your flowers among,'
I wove your blue-bells into garlands wild,
    And woke your echoes with my artless song.
Ah, hills beloved! - your turf, your flowers remain;
    But can the peace to his sad breast restore,
For one poor moment soothe the sense of pain,
    And teach a breaking heart to throb no more?
And you, Aruna! - in the vale below,
    As to the sea your limpid waves you bear,
Can you one kind Lethean cup bestow,
    To drink a long oblivion to my care?
Ah, no! - when all, e'en hope's last ray is gone,
There's no oblivion - but in death alone!-from *Beachy Head*

An early worshipper at Nature's shrine,
I loved her rudest scenes - warrens, and heaths,
And yellow commons, and birch-shaded hollows,
And hedge rows, bordering unfrequented lanes
Bowered with wild roses, and the clasping woodbine
Where purple tassels of the tangling vetch
With bittersweet, and bryony inweave,
And the dew fills the silver bindweed's cups -
I loved to trace the brooks whose humid banks
Nourish the harebell, and the freckled pagil;
And stroll among o'ershadowing woods of beech,
Lending in summer, from the heats of noon
A whispering shade; while haply there reclines

Some pensive lover of uncultured flowers,
Who, from the tumps with bright green mosses clad,
Plucks the wood sorrel, with its light thin leaves,
Heart-shaped, and triply folded; and its root
Creeping like beaded coral; or who there
Gathers, the copse's pride, anemones,
With rays like golden studs on ivory laid
Most delicate; but touched with purple clouds,
Fit crown for April's fair but changeful brow.
Ah! hills so early loved! in fancy still
I breathe your pure keen air; and still behold
Those widely spreading views, mocking alike
The poet and the painter's utmost art.

ANN YEARSLEY
(1749-1806)

Anarchy

Furies! why sleep amid the carnage! – rise!
   Bring up my wolves of war, my pointed spears.
Daggers, yet reeking, banners filled with sighs,
    And paint your cheek with gore, and lave your locks in
                               tears.

On yon white bosom see that happy child!
   Seize it, deface its infant charms! And say,
Anarchy viewed its mingled limbs and smiled.
   Strike the young mother to the earth! – Away!

This is my era! O'er the dead I go!
   From my hot nostrils minute murders fall!
Behind my burning car lurks feeble Woe!
   Filled with my dragon's ire, my slaves for kingdoms call!

Hear them not, Father of the ensanguined race! –
World! Give my monster way! – death! keep thy steady
                  chase!

WILLIAM BLAKE

(1757-1827)

Night

The sun descending in the west,
The evening star does shine;
The birds are silent in their nest,
And I must seek for mine.
The Moon, like a flower,
In heaven's high bower,
With silent delight
Sits and smiles on the night.

Farewell, green fields and happy groves,
Where flocks have took delight.
Where lambs have nibble, silent moves
The feet of angels bright;
Unseen they pour blessing,
And joy without ceasing,
On each bud and blossom,
And each sleeping bosom.

They look in every thoughtless nest,
Where birds are cover'd warm;
They visit caves of every beast,
To keep them all from harm.
If they see any weeping
That should have been sleeping,
They pour sleep on their head,
And sit down by their bed.
When wolves and tigers howl for prey,
They pitying stand and weep;

Seeking to drive their thirst away,
And keep them from the sheep.
But if they rush dreadful,
The angels, most heedful,
Receive each mild spirit,
New worlds to inherit.

And there the lion's ruddy eyes
Shall flow with tears of gold,
And pitying the tender cries,
And walking round the fold,
Saying: 'Wrath, by His meekness,
And, by His health, sickness
Is driven away.
From our immortal day.

'And now beside thee, bleating lamb,
I can lie down and sleep;
Or think on Him who bore thy name,
Graze after thee and weep.
For, wash'd in life's river,
My bright mane for ever
Shall shine like the gold
As I guard o'er the fold.'

Song

Fresh from the dewy hill, the merry year
Smiles on my head, and mounts his flaming car;
Round my young brows the laurel wreathes a shade,
And rising glories beam around my head.

My feet are wing'd, while o'er the dewy lawn,
I meet my maiden, risen like the morn:
Oh bless those holy feet, like angels' feet;
Oh bless those limbs, beaming with heav'nly light!

Like as an angel glitt'ring in the sky,
In times of innocence, and holy joy;
The joyful shepherd stops his grateful song,
To hear the music of an angel's tongue.

So when she speaks, the voice of Heaven I hear
So when we walk, nothing impure comes near;
Each field seems Eden, and each calm retreat;
Each village seems the haunt of holy feet.

But that sweet village where my black-ey'd maid,
Closes her eyes in sleep beneath night's shade:
Whene'er I enter, more than mortal fire
Burns in my soul, and does my song inspire.

Hear the Voice

Hear the voice of the Bard,
Who present, past, and future, sees;
Whose ears have heard
The Holy Word
That walk'd among the ancient trees;

Calling the lapsèd soul,
And weeping in the evening dew;
That might control
The starry pole,
And fallen, fallen light renew!

'O Earth, O Earth, return!
Arise from out the dewy grass!
Night is worn,
And the morn
Rises from the slumbrous mass.

'Turn away no more;
Why wilt thou turn away?
The starry floor,
The watery shore,
Is given thee till the break of day.'

Mad Song

The wild winds weep,
    And the night is a-cold;
Come hither, Sleep,
    And my griefs enfold! . . .
But lo! the morning peeps
    Over the eastern steeps,
And the rustling beds of dawn
The earth do scorn.

Lo! to the vault
    Of pavèd heaven,
With sorrow fraught,
    My notes are driven:
They strike the ear of Night,
    Make weak the eyes of Day;
They make mad the roaring winds,
And with the tempests play,

Like a fiend in a cloud,
    With howling woe
After night I do crowd
    And with night will go;
I turn my back to the east
    From whence comforts have increased;
For light doth seize my brain
With frantic pain.

Songs of Innocence

Piping down the valleys wild,
Piping songs of peasant glee,
On a cloud I saw a child,
And he, laughing, said to me:

'Pipe a song about a lamb!'
So I piped with merry cheer.
'Piper, pipe that song again;'
So I piped: he wept to hear.

'Drop thy pipe, thy happy pipe;
Sing thy songs of happy cheer!'
So I sang the same again,
While he wept with joy to hear.

'Piper, sit thee down and write
In a book, that all may read.'
So he vanished from my sight;
And I plucked a hollow reed,

And I made a rural pen,
And I stain'd the water clear,
And I wrote my happy songs
Every child may joy to hear.

To the Evening Star

Thou fair-hair'd angel of the evening,
Now, whilst the sun rests on the mountains, light
Thy bright torch of love; thy radiant crown
Put on, and smile upon our evening bed!
Smile on our loves, and while thou drawest the
Blue curtains of the sky, scatter thy silver dew
On every flower that shuts its sweet eyes
In timely sleep. Let thy west wind sleep on
The lake; speak silence with thy glimmering eyes,
And wash the dusk with silver. Soon, full soon,
Dost thou withdraw; then the wolf rages wide,
And then the lion glares through the dun forest:
The fleeces of our flocks are cover'd with
Thy sacred dew: protect them with thine influence!

MARY ROBINSON

(1758-1800)

Sonnet: To Liberty

Oh! liberty! transcendent and sublime!
   Born on the mountain's solitary crest;
Nature thy nurse, thy fire unconquered Time,
   Truth, the pure inmate of thy glowing breast!
Oft dost thou wander by the billowy deep,
   Scattering the sands that bind the level shore,
Or, towering, brave the desolating roar
   That bids the tyrant tempest lash the steep!
'Tis thine, when sanguinary dæmons lour,
   Amidst the thickening hosts to force thy way;
To quell the minion of oppressive power,
   And shame the vaunting nothings of a day!
Still shall the human mind thy name adore,
   Till chaos reigns – and worlds shall be no more!

from *To the Poet Coleridge*

Spirit divine! with thee I'll trace,
Imagination's boundless space!
With thee, beneath thy 'sunny dome,'
I'll listen to the minstrel's lay,
Hymning the gradual close of day,
In 'caves of ice' enchanted roam,
Where on the glittering entrance plays
The moon's-beam with its silvery rays;
Or, when the glassy stream,
That through the deep dell flows,
Flashes the noon's hot beam,
The noon's hot beam, that midway shows
Thy flaming temple, studded o'er
With all Peruvia's lustrous store!
There will I trace the circling bounds
Of thy New Paradise, extended,
And listen to the awful sounds
Of winds, and foamy torrents blended!

Stanzas Written After Successive Nights
of Melancholy Dream

Ye airy Phantoms, by whose power
　　Night's curtains spread a deeper shade;
Who, prowling in the murky hour,
　　The weary sense with spells invade;
Why round the fibres of my brain,
　　Such desolating miseries fling,
And, with new scenes of mental pain,
Chase from my languid eye, sleep's balm-dispensing wing?

Ah! why, when o'er the darkened globe
　　All Nature's children sink to rest –
Why, wrapped in horrors ghastly robe,
　　With shadowy hand assail my breast?
Why conjure up a tribe forlorn,
　　To menace, where I bend my way?
Why round my pillow plant the thorn,
　　Or fix the Demon dire, in terrible array?

Why, when the busy day is o'er –
　　A day, perhaps, of *tender thought* –
Why bid my eager gaze explore
　　New prospect, with new anguish fraught?
Why bid my maddening sense decry
　　The Form, in silence I adore!
His magic mile! his murderous eye!
Then bid me wake to prove, the fond illusion o'er!

When, feverish with the throbs of pain,
　　And bathed with many a trickling tear,
I close my cheated eyes again,
　　Despair's wild band are hovering near;

Now borne upon the yelling blast,
  O'er craggy Peaks I bend my flight;
Now, on the yawning Ocean cast,
I plunge unfathomed depth, amid the shades of night!

Or, borne upon the billow's Ire,
  O'er the vast waste of water's drear,
Where shipwrecked Mariners expire,
  No friend their dying plaints to hear,
I view far off the craggy cliff,
  Whose white top mingles with the skies;
While, at its base, the shattered Skiff,
Washed by the foaming wave, in many a fragment lies.

Oft, when the Morning's gaudy beam
  My lattices gild with sparkling light,
O'erwhelmed with agonizing dreams,
  And bound in spells of Fancied Night,
I start, convulsive, wild, distraught!
  By some pale Murderer's poignard pressed,
Or by the grinning Phantom aught,
Wake from the maddening grasp with horror-freezing breast!

Then, down my cold and pallid cheek,
  The mingling tears of joy and grief,
The soul's tumultuous feelings speak,
  And yield the struggling heart relief;
I smile to know the danger past!
  But soon the radiant moment flies;
Soon is the transient Day o'ercast,
And hope steels trembling from my languid eyes!

If Thus, for Moments of repose,
  Whole Hours of misery I must know;
If, when each sunny day shall close,

I must each gleam of Peace forgo!
If, for one Little Morn of Mirth,
    This breast must feel long nights of pain;
  Oh! Life, thy joys are nothing worth;
Then let me sing to rest - and never wake again!

HELEN MARIA WILLIAMS
(1761-1827)

Sonnet: To the Torrid Zone

Pathway of light! o'er thy empurpled zone
With lavish charms perennial summer strays;
Soft 'midst thy spicy groves the zephyr plays,
While far around the rich perfumes are thrown;
The amadavid-bird for the alone
Spreads his gay plumes that catch thy vivid ray;
For thee the gems with liquid lustre blaze,
And nature's various wealth is all thy own.
But ah! not thine is twilight's doubtful gloom.
Those mild gradations, mingling day with night;
Here, instant darkness shroud thy genial bloom,
Nor leave my pensive soul that lingering light,
When musing memory would each trace resume
Of fading pleasures in successive flight.

BARBARA HOOLE

(1770-1844)

Sonnet, Composed on the Banks of Ullswater

Ah, scenes! beloved by Fancy's beaming eye,
    Enthusiast sweet, that o'er the mountain wild
Breathes in soft ecstasy the rapturous sigh,
    Or sings exulting through the smiling vale;
Now through the dark glen wandering madly mild,
    Or slowly sauntering through the flowery dale:
In each kind breeze that curl the dimpling lake,
    Each orient beam that gilds the rock's bold brow,
She feels young Genius in her bosom wake,
    And mental morn's resplendent beauties glow.
Blessed ray of heaven, which bids the soul inhale
    Whatev'r of good delighted sense portrays,
Pours from each rill and wafts from every gale
    Imagination's intellectual blaze!

WILLIAM WORDSWORTH
(1770-1850)

from *Lines Composed a Few Miles Above Tintern Abbey*

...For I have learned
To look on nature, not as in the hour
Of thoughtless youth; but hearing oftentimes
The still, sad music of humanity,
Nor harsh nor grating, though of ample power
To chasten and subdue. And I have felt
A presence that disturbs me with the joy
Of elevated thoughts; a sense sublime
Of something far more deeply interfused,
Whose dwelling is the light of setting suns,
And the round ocean and the living air,
And the blue sky, and in the mind of man:
A motion and a spirit, that impels
All thinking things, all objects of all thought,
And rolls through all things. Therefore am I still
A lover of the meadows and the woods,
And mountains; and of all that we behold
From this green earth; of all the mighty world
Of eye, and ear, - both what they half create,
And what perceive; well pleased to recognize
In nature and the language of the sense,
The anchor of my purest thoughts, the nurse,
The guide, the guardian of my heart, and soul
Of all my moral being.

from *Ode: Intimations of Immortality From Recollection of Early Childhood*

O joy! that in our embers
Is something that doth live,
That nature yet remembers
What was so fugitive!
The thought of our past years in me doth breed
Perpetual benediction: not indeed
For that which is most worthy to be blest;
Delight and liberty, the simple creed
Of Childhood, whether busy or at rest,
With new-fledged hope still fluttering in his breast: -
Not for these I raise
The song of thanks and praise;
But for those obstinate questionings
Of sense and outward things,
Fallings from us, vanishings;
Blank misgivings of a Creature
Moving about in worlds not realized,
High instincts before which our mortal Nature
Did tremble like a guilty Thing surprised:
But for those first affections,
Those shadowy recollections,
Which, be they what they may,
Are yet the fountain light of all our day,
Are yet a master light of all our seeing;
Upholds us, cherish, and have power to make
Our noisy years seem moments in the being
Of the eternal Silence: truths that wake,
To perish never;
Which neither listlessness, nor mad endeavour,
Nor Man nor Boy,
Not all that is at enmity with joy,

Can utterly abolish or destroy!
        Hence in a season of calm weather
        Though inland far we be,
Our Souls have sight of that immortal sea
        Which brought us thither,
And see the Children sport upon the shore,
And hear the mighty waters rolling evermore.

Then sing, ye Birds, sing, sing a joyous song!
        And let the young Lambs bound
        As to the tabor's sound!
We in thought will join your throng,
        Ye that pipe and ye that play,
        Ye that through your hearts today
        Feel the gladness of the May!
What though the radiance which was once so bright
Be now for ever taken from my sight,
        Though nothing can bring back the hour
Of splendour in the grass, of glory in the flower;
        We will grieve not, rather find
        Strength in what remains behind;
        In the primal sympathy
        Which having been must ever be;
        In the soothing thoughts that spring
        Out of human suffering;
        In the faith that looks through death,
In years that bring the philosophic mind.

And O, ye Fountains, Meadows, Hills, and Groves,
Forbode not any severing of our loves!
Yet in my heart of hearts I feel your might;
I only have relinquished one delight
To live beneath your more habitual sway.
I love the Brooks which down their channels fret,
Even more than when I tripped lightly as they;

The innocent brightness of a new-born Day
               Is lovely yet;
The Clouds that gather round the setting sun
Do take a sober colouring from an eye
That hath kept watch o'er man's mortality;
Another race hath been. And other palms are won.
Thanks to the human heart by which we live,
Thanks to its tenderness, its joys, and fears,
To me the meanest flower that blows can give
Thoughts that do often lie too deep for tears.

from *Lucy*

She dwelt among the untrodden ways
    Beside the springs of Dove,
A Maid whom there were none to praise
    And very few to love.

A violet by a mossy stone
    Half hidden from the eye!
Fair as a star, when only one
    Is shining in the sky.

She lived unknown, and few could know
    When Lucy ceased to be;
But she is in her grave, and oh,
    The difference to me!

"I Wanderered Lonely As a Cloud"

I wandered lonely as a cloud
That floats on high o'er vales and hills,
When all at once I saw a crowd,
A host, of golden daffodils;
Beside the lake, beneath the trees,
Fluttering and dancing in the breeze.

Continuous as the stars that shine
And twinkle on the milky way,
They stretched in never-ending line
Along the margin of the bay:
Ten thousand saw I at a glance,
Tossing their heads in sprightly dance.

The waves beside them danced; but they
Out-did the sparkling waves in glee
A poet could not but be gay,
In such a jocund company
I gazed – and gazed – but little thought
What wealth the show to me had brought:

For oft, when on my couch I lie
In vacant or in pensive mood,
They flash upon that inward eye
Which is the bliss of solitude;
And then my heart with pleasure fills,
And dances with the daffodils.

Evening On Calais Beach

It is a beauteous evening, calm and free,
    The holy time is quiet as a Nun
    Breathless with adoration; the broad sun
Is sinking down in its tranquility;
The gentleness of heaven broods o'er the sea:
    Listen! the mighty Being is awake,
    And doth with his eternal motion make
A sound like thunder - everlastingly.
Dear Child! dear Girl! that walkest with me here,
    If thou appear untouch'd by solemn thought,
    Thy nature is not therefore less divine:
Thou liest in Abraham's bosom all the year;
    And worshipp'st at the Temple's inner shrine,
    God being with thee when we know it not.

Perfect Woman

She was a phantom of delight
When first she gleam'd upon my sight;
A lovely apparition, sent
To be a moment's ornament;
Her eyes as stars of twilight fair;
Like twilight's, too, her dusky hair;
But all things else about her drawn
From May-time and the cheerful dawn;
A dancing shape, an image gay,
To haunt, to startle, and waylay.

I saw her upon nearer view,
A Spirit, yet a Woman too!
Her household motions light and free,
And steps of virgin liberty;
A countenance in which did meet
Sweet records, promises as sweet;
A creature not too bright or good
For human nature's daily food;
For transient sorrows, simple wiles,
Praise, blame, love, kisses, tears, and smiles.

And now I see with eye serene
The very pulse of the machine;
A being breathing thoughtful breath,
A traveller between life and death;
The reason firm, the temperate will,
Endurance, foresight, strength, and skill;
A perfect Woman, nobly plann'd,
To warn, to comfort, and command;
And yet a Spirit still, and bright
With something of angelic light.

DOROTHY WORDSWORTH
(1771-1855)

Floating Island at Hawkshead,
An Incident in the Schemes of Nature

Harmonious powers with Nature work
On sky, earth, river, lake, and sea:
Sunshine and storm, whirlwind and breeze
All in one duteous task agree.

Once did I see a slip of earth,
By throbbing waves long undermined,
Loosed from its hold; – how no one knew
But all might see it float, obedient to the wind.

Might see it, from the verdant shore
Dissevered float upon the lake,
Float, with its crest of trees adorned
On which the warbling birds their pastime take.

Food, shelter, safety there they find
There berries ripen, flowerets bloom;
There insects live their lives – and die:
A people world it is; – in size a tiny room.

And thus through many seasons' space
This little island may survive
But Nature, though we mark her not,
Will take away – may cease to give.

Perchance when you are wandering forth
Upon some vacant sunny day

Without an object, hope, or fear,
Thither your eyes may turn - the isle is passed away.

Buried beneath the glittering lake!
Its place no longer to be found,
Yet the lost fragment shall remain,
To fertilize some other ground.

SAMUEL TAYLOR COLERIDGE
(1772-1834)

This Lime-Tree Bower My Prison

Well, they are gone, and here must I remain,
This lime-tree bower my prison! I have lost
Beauties and feelings, such as would have been
Most sweet to my remembrance even when age
Had dimmed mine eyes to blindness! They, meanwhile,
Friends, whom I never more may meet again,
On springy heath, along the hill-top edge,
Wander in gladness, and wind down, perchance,
To that still roaring dell, of which I told;
The roaring dell, o'erwooded, narrow, deep,
And only speckled by the mid-day sun;
Where its slim trunk the ash from rock to rock
Flings arching like a bridge; – that branchless ash,
Unsunned and damp, whose few poor yellow leaves
Ne'er tremble in the gale, yet tremble still,
Fanned by the waterfall! and there my friends
Behold the dark green file of long lank weeds,
That all at once (a most fantastic sight!)
Still nod and drip beneath the dripping edge
Of the blue clay-stone.

               Now, my friends emerge
Beneath the wide wide Heaven – and view again
The many-steepled tract magnificent
Of hilly fields and meadows, and the sea,
With some fair hark, perhaps, whose sails light up
The slip of smooth clear blue betwixt two Isles
Of purple shadow! Yes! they wander on

In gladness all; but thou, methinks, most glad,
My gentle-hearted Charles! for thou hast pined
And hungered after Nature, many a year,
In the great City pent, winning thy way
With sad yet patient soul, Behind the western ridge, thou glorious
                                                    sun!

Shine in the slant beams of the sinking orb,
Ye purple heath-flowers! richlier burn, ye clouds!
Live in the yellow light, ye distant groves!
And kindle, thou blue ocean! So my Friend
Struck with deep joy may stand, as I have stood,
Silent with swimming sense; yes, gazing round
On the wide landscape, gaze till all doth seem
Less gross than bodily; and of such hues
As veil the Almighty Spirit, when yet he makes
Spirits perceive his presence.
                          A delight
Comes sudden on my heart, and I am glad
As I myself were there! Nor in this bower,
This little lime-tree bower, have I not mark'd
Much that has sooth'd me. Pale beneath the blaze
Hung the transparent foliage; and I watch'd
Some broad and sunny leaf, and lov'd to see
The shadow of the leaf and stem above
Dappling its sunshine! And that walnut-tree
Was richly ting'd, and a deep radiance lay
Full on the ancient ivy, which usurps
Those fronting elms, and now, with blackest mass
Makes their dark branches gleam a lighter hue
Through the late twilight: and though now the bat
Wheels silent by, and not a swallow twitters,
Yet still the solitary humble-bee
Sings in the bean-flower! Henceforth I shall know
That Nature ne'er deserts the wise and pure;
No plot so narrow, be but Nature there,

No waste so vacant, but may well employ
Each faculty of sense, and keep the heart
Awake to Love and Beauty! and sometimes
'Tis well to be bereft of promis'd good,
That we may lift the soul and contemplate
With lively joy the joys we cannot share.
My gentle-hearted Charles! when the last rook
Beat its straight path along the dusky air
Homewards, I blest it! deeming its black wing
(Now a dim speck, now vanishing in light)
Had cross'd the mighty Orb's dilated glory,
While thou stood'st gazing; or, when all was still,
Flew creaking o'er thy head, and had a charm
For thee, my gentle-hearted Charles, to whom
No sound is dissonant which tells of life.

from *Dejection: A Letter*

Well! if the Bard was weatherwise, who made
The grand old Ballad of Sir Patrick Spence,
This Night, so tranquil now, will not go hence
Unrous'd by winds, that ply a busier trade
Than that, which moulds yon clouds in lazy flakes,
Or the dull sobbing Draft, that drones and rakes
Upon the Strings of this Eolian Lute,
Which better far were mute.
For, lo! the New Moon, winter-bright!
And o'erspread with phantom Light
(With swimming phantom Light o'erspread
But rimm'd and circled with a silver Thread)
I see the Old Moon in her Lap, foretelling
The coming-on of Rain and squally Blast –
O! Sara! that the Gust ev'n now were swelling,
And the slant Night-shower driving loud and fast!
·

I feel my spirit moved.
And whereso'er thou be,
O Sister! O Beloved!
Those dear mild Eyes, that see
Even now the Heaven, *I* see –
There is a Prayer in them! It is for *me* –
And I, dear Sara, *I* am blessing *thee*!
·

O Sara! we receive but what we give,
And in *our* life alone does Nature live:
Our's is her Wedding Garment, our's her Shroud –
And would we aught behold of higher Worth
Than that inanimate cold World allow'd
To that poor loveless ever anxious Crowd,
Ah! from the Soul itself must issue forth

A Light, a glory, and a luminous Cloud
Enveloping the Earth!
And from the Soul itself must there be sent
A Sweet and potent Voice, of its own Birth,
Of all sweet Sounds, the Life and Element.
O pure of Heart! thou need'st not ask of me
What this strong music in the Soul may be,
What and wherein it doth exist,
This Light, this Glory, this fair luminous Mist,
This beautiful and beauty-making Power!
Joy, innocent Sara! Joy, that ne'er was given
Save to the pure, and in their purest Hour,
Joy, Sara! is the Spirit and the Power,
That wedding Nature to use gives in Dower
    A new Earth and new Heaven,
Undreamt of by the Sensual and the Proud!
Joy is that strong Voice, Joy that luminous Cloud –
    We, we ourselves rejoice!
And thence flows all that charms or ear or sight,
All melodies, the Echoes of that Voice,
All Colours a Suffusion of that Light.
Sister and Friend of my devoutest Choice
Thou being innocent and full of love,
And nested with the Darlings of thy Love,
And feeling in thy Soul, Heart, Lips, and Arms
Even what the conjugal and mother Dove,
That borrows genial Warmth from those she warms,
Feels in the thrill'd wings, blessedly outspread –
Thou free'd awhile from Cares and human read
By the Immenseness of the Good and Fair
    Which thou seest everywhere –
Thus, thus, should'st thou rejoice!
To thee would all things live from Pole to Pole;
Their Life the Eddying of thy living Soul –
O dear! O Innocent! O full of Love!

A very Friend! A sister of my Choice –
O dear, as Light and Impulse from above,
Thus may'st thou ever, evermore rejoice!

The Nightingale

A conversation poem, April 1798

No cloud, no relique of the sunken day
Distinguishes the West, no long thin slip
Of sullen light, no obscure trembling hues.
Come, we will rest on this old mossy bridge!
You see the glimmer of the stream beneath,
But hear no murmuring: it flows silently,
O'er its soft bed of verdure. All is still,
A balmy night! and though the stars be dim,
Yet let us think upon the vernal showers
That gladden the green earth, and we shall find
A pleasure in the dimness of the stars.
And hark! the Nightingale begins its song,
'Most musical, most melancholy' bird!
A melancholy bird! Oh! idle thought!
In nature there is nothing melancholy.
But some night-wandering man whose heart was pierced
With the remembrance of a grievous wrong,
Or slow distemper, or neglected loved,
(And so, poor wretch! filled all things with himself,
And made all gentle sounds tell back the tale
Of his own sorrow) he, and such as he,
First named these notes a melancholy strain
And many a poet echoes the conceit;
Poet who hath been building up the rhyme
When he had better far have stretched his limbs
Beside a brook in mossy forest-dell,
By sun or moonlight, to the influxes
Of shapes and sounds and shifting elements
Surrendering his whole spirit, of his song
And of his fame forgetful! so his fame

Should share in Nature's immortality,
A venerable thing! and so his song
Should make all Nature lovelier, and itself
Be loved like Nature! But 'twill not be so;
And youths and maidens most poetical,
Who lost the deepening twilights of the spring
In ballrooms and hot theatres, they still
Full of meek sympathy must heave their sighs
O'er Philomela's pity-pleading strains.

My Friend, and thou, our Sister! we have learnt
A different lore: we may not thus profane
Nature's sweet voices, always full of love
And joyance! 'Tis the merry Nightingale
That crowds, and hurries, and precipitates
With fast thick warble his delicious notes,
As he were fearful that an April night
Would be too short for him to utter forth
His love-chant, and disburthen his full soul
Of all his music!

        And I know a grove
Of large extent, hard by a castle huge,
Which the great lord inhabits not; and so
This grove is wild with tangling underwood,
And the trim walks are broken up, and grass,
Thin grass and king-cups grow within the paths.
But never elsewhere in one place I knew
So many nightingales; and far and near,
In wood and thicket, over the wide grove,
They answer and provoke each other's song,
With skirmish and capricious passagings,
And murmurs musical and swift jug jug,
And one low piping sound more sweet than all –
Stirring the air with such a harmony,

That should you close your eyes, you might almost
Forget it was not day! On moonlit bushes,
Whose dewy leaflets are but half disclosed,
You may perchance behold them on the twigs,
Their bright, bright eyes, their eyes both bright and full,
Glistening, while many a glow-worm in the shade
Lights up her love-torch.

       A most gentle Maid,
Who dwelleth in her hospitable home
Hard by the castle, and at latest eve
(Even like a Lady vowed and dedicate
To something more than Nature in the grove)
Glides through the pathways; she knows all their notes,
That gentle Maid! and oft a moment's space,
What time the moon was lost behind a cloud,
Hath heard a pause of silence; till the moon
Emerging, hath awakened earth and sky
With one sensation, and these wakeful birds
Have all burst forth in choral minstrelsy,
As if some sudden gale had swept at once
A hundred airy harps! And she hath watched
Many a nightingale perched giddily
On blossomy twig still swinging from the breeze,
And to that motion tune his wanton song
Like tipsy joy that reels with tossing head.

  Farewell, O Warbler! till tomorrow eve,
And you, my friends! farewell, a short farewell!
We have been loitering long and pleasantly,
And now for our dear homes. – That strain again!
Full fain it would delay me! My dear babe,
Who, capable of no articulate sound,
Mars all things with his imitative lisp,
How he would place his hand beside his ear,

His little hand, the small forefinger up,
And bid us listen! And I deem it wise
To make him Nature's playmate. He knows well
The evening-star; and once, when he awoke
In most distressful mood (some inward pain
Had made up that strange thing, an infant's dream. -)
I hurried with him to our orchard-plot,
And he beheld the moon, and hushed at once,
Suspends his sobs, and laughs most silently,
While his fair eyes, that swam with undropped tears,
Did glitter in the yellow moon-beam! Well! –
It is a father's tale: But if that Heaven
Should give me life, his childhood shall grow up
Familiar with these songs, that with the night
He may associate joy. – Once more, farewell,
Sweet Nightingale! once more, my friends! farewell.

Frost at Midnight

The Frost performs its secret ministry,
Unhelped by any wind. The owlet's cry
Came loud-and hark, again! loud as before.
The inmates of my cottage, all at rest,
Have left me to that solitude, which suits
Abstruser musings: save that at my side
My cradled infant slumbers peacefully.
'tis calm indeed! so calm, that it disturbs
And vexes meditation with its strange
And extreme silentness. Sea, hill, and wood,
This populous village! Sea, and hill, and wood,
With all the numberless goings-on of life,
Inaudible as dreams! the thin blue flame
Lies on my low-burnt fire, and quivers not;
Only that film, which fluttered on the grate,
Still flutters there, the sole unquiet thing.
Methinks, its motion in this hush of nature
Gives it dim sympathies with me who live,
Making it a companionable form,
Whose puny flaps and freaks the idling Spirit
By its own moods interprets, every where
Echo or mirror seeking of itself,
And makes a toy of Thought.

But O! how oft,
How oft, at school, with most believing mind,
Presageful, have I gazed upon the bars,
To watch that fluttering stranger! and as oft
With unclosed lids, already had I dreamt
Of my sweet birth-place, and the old church-tower,
Whose bells, the poor man's only music, rang
From morn to evening, all the hot Fair-day,

So sweetly, that they stirred and haunted me
With a wild pleasure, falling on mine ear
Most like articulate sounds of things to come!
So gazed I, till the soothing things, I dreamt,
Lulled me to sleep, and sleep prolonged my dreams!
And so I brooded all the following morn,
Awed by the stern preceptor's face, mine eye
Fixed with mock study on my swimming book:
Save if the door half opened, and I snatched
A hasty glance, and still my heart leaped up,
For still I hoped to see the stranger's face,
Townsman, or aunt, or sister more beloved,
My play-mate when we both were clothed alike!

    Dear Babe, that sleepest cradled by my side,
Whose gentle breathings, heard in this deep calm,
Fill up the interspersèd vacancies
And momentary pauses of the thought!
My babe so beautiful! it thrills my heart
With tender gladness, thus to look at thee,
And think that thou shalt learn far other lore,
And in far other scenes! For I was reared
In the great city, pent 'mid cloisters dim,
And saw nought lovely but the sky and stars.
But thou, my babe! shalt wander like a breeze
By lakes and sandy shores, beneath the crags
Of ancient mountain, and beneath the clouds,
Which image in their bulk both lakes and shores
And mountain crags: so shalt thou see and hear
The lovely shapes and sounds intelligible
Of that eternal language, which thy God
Utters, who from eternity doth teach
Himself in all, and all things in himself.
Great universal Teacher! he shall mould
Thy spirit, and by giving make it ask.

Therefore all seasons shall be sweet to thee,
Whether the summer clothe the general earth
With greenness, or the redbreast sit and sing
Betwixt the tufts of snow on the bare branch
Of mossy apple-tree, while the nigh thatch
Smokes in the sun-thaw; whether the eave-drops fall
Heard only in the trances of the blast,
Or if the secret ministry of frost
Shall hang them up in silent icicles,
Quietly shining to the quiet Moon.

Fears in Solitude

WRITTEN IN APRIL 1798, DURING THE
ALARM OF AN INVASION

A green and silent spot, amid the hills,
A small and silent dell! O'er stiller place
No singing sky-lark ever poised himself.
The hills are heathy, save that swelling slope,
Which hath a gay and gorgeous covering on,
All golden with the never-bloomless furze,
Which now blooms most profusely: but the dell,
Bathed by the mist, is fresh and delicate
As vernal corn-field, or the unripe flax,
When, through its half-transparent stalks, at eve,
The level sunshine glimmers with green light.
Oh! 'tis a quiet spirit-healing nook!
Which all, methinks, would love; but chiefly he,
The humble man, who, in his youthful years,
Knew just so much of folly, as had made
His early manhood more securely wise!
Here he might lie on fern or withered heath,
While from the singing lark (that sings unseen
The minstrelsy that solitude loves best),
And from the sun, and from the breezy air,
Sweet influences trembled o'er his frame;
And he, with many feelings, many thoughts,
Made up a meditative joy, and found
Religious meanings in the forms of Nature!
And so, his senses gradually wrapt
In a half sleep, he dreams of better worlds,
And dreaming hears thee still, O singing lark,
That singest like an angel in the clouds!

My God! it is a melancholy thing
For such a man, who would full fain preserve
His soul in calmness, yet perforce must feel
For all his human brethren-O my God!
It weighs upon the heart, that he must think
What uproar and what strife may now be stirring
This way or that way o'er these silent hills –
Invasion, and the thunder and the shout,
And all the crash of onset; fear and rage,
And undetermined conflict-even now,
Even now, perchance, and in his native isle:
Carnage and groans beneath this blessed sun!
We have offended, Oh! my countrymen!
We have offended very grievously,
And been most tyrannous. From east to west
A groan of accusation pierces Heaven!
The wretched plead against us; multitudes
Countless and vehement, the sons of God,
Our brethren! Like a cloud that travels on,
Steamed up from Cairo's swamps of pestilence,
Even so, my countrymen! have we gone forth
And borne to distant tribes slavery and pangs,
And, deadlier far, our vices, whose deep taint
With slow perdition murders the whole man,
His body and his soul! Meanwhile, at home,
All individual dignity and power
Engulfed in Courts, Committees, Institutions,
Associations and Societies,
A vain, speech-mouthing, speech-reporting Guild,
One Benefit-Club for mutual flattery,
We have drunk up, demure as at a grace,
Pollutions from the brimming cup of wealth;
Contemptuous of all honourable rule,
Yet bartering freedom and the poor man's life

For gold, as at a market! The sweet words
Of Christian promise, words that even yet
Might stem destruction, were they wisely preached,
Are muttered o'er by men, whose tones proclaim
How flat and wearisome they feel their trade:
Rank scoffers some, but most too indolent
To deem them falsehoods or to know their truth.
Oh! blasphemous! the Book of Life is made
A superstitious instrument, on which
We gabble o'er the oaths we mean to break;
For all must swear-all and in every place,
College and wharf, council and justice-court;
All, all must swear, the briber and the bribed,
Merchant and lawyer, senator and priest,
The rich, the poor, the old man and the young;
All, all make up one scheme of perjury,
That faith doth reel; the very name of God
Sounds like a juggler's charm; and, bold with joy,
Forth from his dark and lonely hiding-place,
(Portentious sight!) the owlet Atheism,
Sailing on obscene wings athwart the noon,
Drops his blue-fringèd lids, and holds them close,
And hooting at the glorious sun in Heaven,
Cries out, 'Where is it?'

                    Thankless too for peace,
(Peace long preserved by fleets and perilous seas)
Secure from actual warfare, we have loved
To swell the war-whoop, passionate for war!
Alas! for ages ignorant of all
Its ghastlier workings, (famine or blue plague,
Battle, or siege, or flight through wintry snows,)
We, this whole people, have been clamorous
For war and bloodshed; animating sports,
The which we pay for as a thing to talk of,

Spectators and not combatants! No guess
Anticipative of a wrong unfelt,
No speculation on contingency,
However dim and vague, too vague and dim
To yield a justifying cause; and forth,
(Stuffed out with big preamble, holy names,
And adjurations of the God in Heaven,)
We send our mandates for the certain death
Of thousands and ten thousands! Boys and girls,
And women, that would groan to see a child
Pull off an insect's wing, all read of war,
The best amusement for our morning meal!
The poor wretch, who has learnt his only prayers
From curses, and who knows scarcely words enough
To ask a blessing from his Heavenly Father,
Becomes a fluent phraseman, absolute
And technical in victories and defeats,
And all our dainty terms for fratricide;
Terms which we trundle smoothly o'er our tongues
Like mere abstractions, empty sounds to which
We join no feeling and attach no form!
As if the soldier died without a wound;
As if the fibres of this godlike frame
Were gored without a pang; as if the wretch,
Who fell in battle, doing bloody deeds,
Passed off to Heaven, translated and not killed;
As though he had no wife to pine for him,
No God to judge him! Therefore, evil days
Are coming on us, O my countrymen!
And what if all-avenging Providence,
Strong and retributive, should make us know
The meaning of our words, force us to feel
The desolation and the agony
Of our fierce doings?

Spare us yet awhile,
Father and God! O! spare us yet awhile!
Oh! let not English women drag their flight
Fainting beneath the burthen of their babes,
Of the sweet infants, that but yesterday
Laughed at the breast! Sons, brothers, husbands, all
Who ever gazed with fondness on the forms
Which grew up with you round the same fire-side,
And all who ever heard the sabbath-bells
Without the infidel's scorn, make yourselves pure!
Stand forth! be men! repel an impious foe,
Impious and false, a light yet cruel race,
Who laugh away all virtue, mingling mirth
With deeds of murder; and still promising
Freedom, themselves too sensual to be free,
Poison life's amities, and cheat the heart
Of faith and quiet hope, and all that soothes,
And all that lifts the spirit! Stand we forth;
Render them back upon the insulted ocean,
And let them toss as idly on its waves
As the vile sea-weed, which some mountain-blast
Swept from our shores! And oh! may we return
Not with a drunken triumph, but with fear,
Repenting of the wrongs with which we stung
So fierce a foe to frenzy!

                    I have told,
O Britons! O my brethren! I have told
Most bitter truth, but without bitterness.
Nor deem my zeal or factious or mistimed;
For never can true courage dwell with them,
Who, playing tricks with conscience, dare not look
At their own vices. We have been too long
Dupes of a deep delusion! Some, belike,
Groaning with restless enmity, expect

❖ *57*

All change from change of constituted power;
As if a Government had been a robe,
On which our vice and wretchedness were tagged
Like fancy-points and fringes, with the robe
Pulled off at pleasure. Fondly these attach
A radical causation to a few
Poor drudges of chastising Providence,
Who borrow all their hues and qualities
From our own folly and rank wickedness,
Which gave them birth and nursed them. Others, meanwhile,
Dote with a mad idolatry; and all
Who will not fall before their images,
And yield them worship, they are enemies
Even of their country!

           Such have I been deemed –
But, O dear Britain! O my Mother Isle!
Needs must thou prove a name most dear and holy
To me, a son, a brother, and a friend,
A husband, and a father! who revere
All bonds of natural love, and find them all
Within the limits of thy rocky shores.
O native Britain! O my Mother Isle!
How shouldst thou prove aught else but dear and holy
To me, who from thy lakes and mountain-hills,
Thy clouds, thy quiet dales, thy rocks and seas,
Have drunk in all my intellectual life,
All sweet sensations, all ennobling thoughts,
All adoration of God in nature,
All lovely and all honourable things,
Whatever makes this mortal spirit feel
The joy and greatness of its future being?
There lives nor form nor feeling in my soul
Unborrowed from my country! O divine
And beauteous island! thou hast been my sole

And most magnificent temple, in the which
I walk with awe, and sing my stately songs,
Loving the God that made me! –

                        May my fears,
My filial fears, be vain! and may the vaunts
And menace of the vengeful enemy
Pass like the gust, that roared and died away
In the distant tree: which heard, and only heard
In this low dell, bowed not the delicate grass.

   But now the gentle dew-fall sends abroad
The fruit-like perfume of the golden furze:
The light has left the summit of the hill,
Though still a sunny gleam lies beautiful,
Aslant the ivied beacon. Now farewell,
Farewell, awhile, O soft and silent spot!
On the green sheep-track, up the heathy hill,
Homeward I wind my way; and lo! recalled
From bodings that have well-nigh wearied me,
I find myself upon the brow, and pause
Startled! And after lonely sojourning
In such a quiet and surrounded nook,
This burst of prospect, here the shadowy main,
Dim tinted, there the mighty majesty
Of that huge amphitheatre of rich
And elmy fields, seems like society –
Conversing with the mind, and giving it
A livelier impulse and a dance of thought!
And now, belovèd Stowey! I behold
Thy church-tower, and, methinks, the four huge elms
Clustering, which mark the mansion of my friend;
And close behind them, hidden from my view,
Is my own lowly cottage, where my babe
And my babe's mother dwell in peace! With light

And quickened footsteps thitherward I tend,
Remembering thee, O green and silent dell!
And grateful, that by nature's quietness
And solitary musings, all my heart
Is softened, and made worthy to indulge
Love, and the thoughts that yearn for human kind.

The AEolian Harp

COMPOSED AUGUST 20TH, 1795
AT CLEVEDON, SOMERSETSHIRE

My pensive Sara! thy soft cheek reclined
Thus on mine arm, most soothing sweet it is
To sit beside our Cot, our Cot o'ergrown
With white-flower'd Jasmin, and the broad-leav'd Myrtle,
(Meet emblems they of Innocence and Love!)
And watch the clouds, that late were rich with light,
Slow saddenning round, and mark the star of eve
Serenely brilliant (such should Wisdom be)
Shine opposite! How exquisite the scents
Snatch'd from yon bean-field! and the world so hush'd!
The stilly murmur of the distant Sea
Tells us of silence.

            And that simplest Lute,
Plac'd length-ways in the clasping casement, hark!
How by the desultory breeze caress'd,
Like some coy maid half-yielding to her lover,
It pours such sweet upbraiding, as must needs
Tempt to repeat the wrong! And now, its strings
Boldlier swept, the long sequacious notes
Over delicious surges sink and rise,
Such a soft floating witchery of sound
As twilight Elfins make, when they at eve
Voyage on gentle gales from Faery-Land,
Where Melodies round honey-dropping flowers,
Footless and wild, like birds of Paradise,
Nor pause, nor perch, hovering on untam'd wing!
O! the one Life within us and abroad,

Which meets all motion and becomes its soul,
A light in sound, a sound-like power in light,
Rhythm in all thought, and joyance every where –
Methinks, it should have been impossible
Not to love all things in a world so fill'd;
Where the breeze warbles, and the mute still air
Is Music slumbering on her instrument.

And thus, my Love! as on the midway slope
Of yonder hill I stretch my limbs at noon,
Whilst thro' my half-clos'd eye-lids I behold
The sunbeams dance, like diamonds, on the main,
And tranquil muse upon tranquility;
Full many a thought uncall'd and undetain'd,
And many idle flitting phantasies,
Traverse my indolent and passive brain,
As wild and various, as the random gales
That swell and flutter on this subject Lute!

And what if all of animated nature
Be but organic Harps diversly fram'd,
That tremble into thought, as o'er them sweeps
Plastic and vast, one intellectual breeze,
At once the Soul of each, and God of all?

But thy more serious eye a mild reproof
Darts, O belovèd Woman! nor such thoughts
Dim and unhallow'd dost thou not reject,
And biddest me walk humbly with my God.
Meek Daughter in the Family of Christ!
Well hast thou said and holily disprais'd
These shapings of the unregenerate mind;
Bubbles that glitter as they rise and break
On vain Philosophy's aye-babbling spring.
For never guiltless may I speak of him,

The Incomprehensible! save when with awe
I praise him, and with Faith that inly feels;
Who with his saving mercies healèd me,
A sinful and most miserable man,
Wilder'd and dark, and gave me to possess
Peace, and this Cot, and thee, heart-honour'd Maid!

GEORGE GORDON, LORD BYRON

(1788-1824)

from *Childe Harold's Pilgrimage (Canto II)*

Come, blue-eyed maid of heaven! – but thou, alas!
Didst never yet one mortal song inspire –
Goddess of Wisdom! here thy temple was,
And is, despite of war and wasting fire,
And years, that bade thy worship to expire:
But worse than steel, and flame, and ages slow,
Is the dread sceptre and dominion dire
Of men who never felt the sacred glow,
That thoughts of thee and thine on polish'd breasts bestow.

Ancient of days! august Athena! where,
Where are thy men of might? thy grand in soul?
Gone – glimmering through the dream of things that were:
First in the race that led to Glory's goal,
They won, and pass'd away – is this the whole?
A school-boy's tale, the wonder of an hour!
The warrior's weapons and the sophist's stole
Are sought in vain, and o'er each mouldering tower,
Dim with the mist of years, grey flits the shadow of power.

Son of the morning, rise! approach you here!
Come – but molest not yon defenceless urn:
Look on this spot – A nation's sepulchre!
Abode of gods, whose shrines no longer burn.
Even gods must yield – religions take their turn:
'Twas Jove's – 'tis Mahomet's – and other creeds
Will rise with other years, till man shall learn
Vainly his incense soars, his victim bleeds;

Poor child of Doubt and Death, whose hope is built on reeds.

Bound to the earth, he lifts his eye to heaven –
Is't not enough, unhappy thing! to know
Thou art? Is this a boon so kindly given,
That being, thou wouldst be again, and go,
Thou know'st not, reck'st not to what region, so
On earth no more, but mingled with the skies?
Still wilt thou dream on future joy and woe?
Regard and weigh yon dust before it flies:
That little urn saith more than thousand homilies.

Or burst the vanish'd Hero's lofty mount;
Far on the solitary shore he sleeps:
He fell, and falling nations mourn'd around;
But now not one of saddening thousands weeps,
Nor warlike worshipper his vigil keeps
Where demi-gods appear'd, as records tell.
Remove yon skull from out the scatter'd heaps:
Is that a temple where a God may dwell?
Why ev'n the worm at last disdains her shatter'd cell!

Look on its broken arch, its ruin'd wall,
Its chambers desolate, and portals foul:
Yes, this was once Ambition's airy hall,
The dome of Thought, the palace of the Soul:
Behold through each lacklustre, eyeless hole,
The gay recess of Wisdom and of Wit
And Passion's host, that never brook'd control:
Can all, saint, sage, or sophist ever writ,
People this lonely tower, this tenement refit?

Well didst thou speak, Athena's wisest son!
'All that we know is, nothing can be known.'
Why should we shrink from that we cannot shun?

Each has his pang, but feeble sufferers groan
With brain-born dreams of evil all their own.
Pursue what Chance or Fate proclaimeth best;
Peace waits us on the shores of Acheron:
There no forc'd banquet claims the sated guest,
But Silence spreads the couch of ever welcome rest.

"She Walks in Beauty"

She walks in beauty, like the night
   Of cloudless climes and starry skies;
And all that's best of dark and bright
   Meet in her aspect and her eyes:
Thus mellow'd to that tender light
   Which heaven to gaudy day denies.

One shade the more, one ray the less,
   Had half impair'd the nameless grace
Which waves in every raven tress,
   Or softly lightens o'er her face;
Where thoughts serenely sweet express
   How pure, how dear their dwelling place.

And on that cheek, and o'er that brow,
   So soft, so calm, yet eloquent,
The smiles that win, the tints that glow,
   But tell of days in goodness spent,
A mind at peace with all below,
   A heart whose love is innocent!

"When We Two Parted"

When we two parted
   In silence and tears,
Half broken-hearted
   To sever for years,
Pale grew thy cheek and cold,
   Colder thy kiss;
Truly that hour foretold
   Sorrow to this.

The dew of the morning
   Sunk chill on my brow–
It felt like the warning
   Of what I feel now.
Thy vows are all broken,
   And light is thy fame:
I hear thy name spoken,
   And share in its shame.

They name thee before me,
   A knell to mine ear;
A shudder comes o'er me –
   Why wert thou so dear?
They know not I knew thee,
   Who knew thee too well:
Lond, long shall I rue thee,
   Too deeply to tell.

I secret we met –
   I silence I grieve,
That thy heart could forget,
   Thy spirit deceive.
If I should meet thee

After long years,
How should I greet thee?
With silence and tears.

Darkness

I had a dream, which was not all a dream.
The bright sun was extinguish'd, and the stars
Did wander darkling in the eternal space,
Rayless, and pathless, and the icy earth
Swung blind and blackening in the moonless air;
Morn came and went - and came, and brought no day,
And men forgot their passions in the dread
Of this their desolation; and all hearts
Were chill'd into a selfish prayer for light:
And they did live by watchfires - and the thrones,
The palaces of crowned kings - the huts,
The habitations of all things which dwell,
Were burnt for beacons; cities were consum'd,
And men were gather'd round their blazing homes
To look once more into each other's face;
Happy were those who dwelt within the eye
Of the volcanos, and their mountain-torch:
A fearful hope was all the world contain'd;
Forests were set on fire - but hour by hour
They fell and faded - and the crackling trunks
Extinguish'd with a crash - and all was black.
The brows of men by the despairing light
Wore an unearthly aspect, as by fits
The flashes fell upon them; some lay down
And hid their eyes and wept; and some did rest
Their chins upon their clenched hands, and smil'd;
And others hurried to and fro, and fed
Their funeral piles with fuel, and look'd up
With mad disquietude on the dull sky,
The pall of a past world; and then again
With curses cast them down upon the dust,
And gnash'd their teeth and howl'd: the wild birds shriek'd

And, terrified, did flutter on the ground,
And flap their useless wings; the wildest brutes
Came tame and tremulous; and vipers crawl'd
And twin'd themselves among the multitude,
Hissing, but stingless - they were slain for food.
And War, which for a moment was no more,
Did glut himself again: a meal was bought
With blood, and each sate sullenly apart
Gorging himself in gloom: no love was left;
All earth was but one thought - and that was death
Immediate and inglorious; and the pang
Of famine fed upon all entrails - men
Died, and their bones were tombless as their flesh;
The meagre by the meagre were devour'd,
Even dogs assail'd their masters, all save one,
And he was faithful to a corse, and kept
The birds and beasts and famish'd men at bay,
Till hunger clung them, or the dropping dead
Lur'd their lank jaws; himself sought out no food,
But with a piteous and perpetual moan,
And a quick desolate cry, licking the hand
Which answer'd not with a caress - he died.
The crowd was famish'd by degrees; but two
Of an enormous city did survive,
And they were enemies: they met beside
The dying embers of an altar-place
Where had been heap'd a mass of holy things
For an unholy usage; they rak'd up,
And shivering scrap'd with their cold skeleton hands
The feeble ashes, and their feeble breath
Blew for a little life, and made a flame
Which was a mockery; then they lifted up
Their eyes as it grew lighter, and beheld
Each other's aspects - saw, and shriek'd, and died -
Even of their mutual hideousness they died,

Unknowing who he was upon whose brow
Famine had written Fiend. The world was void,
The populous and the powerful was a lump,
Seasonless, herbless, treeless, manless, lifeless –
A lump of death – a chaos of hard clay.
The rivers, lakes and ocean all stood still,
And nothing stirr'd within their silent depths;
Ships sailorless lay rotting on the sea,
And their masts fell down piecemeal: as they dropp'd
They slept on the abyss without a surge –
The waves were dead; the tides were in their grave,
The moon, their mistress, had expir'd before;
The winds were wither'd in the stagnant air,
And the clouds perish'd; Darkness had no need
Of aid from them – She was the Universe.

Prometheus

Titan! to whose immortal eyes
The sufferings of mortality,
Seen in their sad reality,
Were not as things that gods despise;
What was thy pity's recompense?
A silent suffering, and intense;
The rock, the vulture, and the chain,
All that the proud can feel of pain,
The agony they do not show,
The suffocating sense of woe,
Which speaks but in its loneliness,
And then is jealous lest the sky
Should have a listener, nor will sigh
Until its voice is echoless.

Titan! to thee the strife was given
Between the suffering and the will,
Which torture where they cannot kill;
And the inexorable Heaven,
And the deaf tyranny of Fate,
The ruling principle of Hate,
Which for its pleasure doth create
The things it may annihilate,
Refus'd thee even the boon to die:
The wretched gift Eternity
Was thine - and thou hast borne it well.
All that the Thunderer wrung from thee
Was but the menace which flung back
On him the torments of thy rack;
The fate thou didst so well foresee,
But would not to appease him tell;
And in thy Silence was his Sentence,

And in his Soul a vain repentance,
And evil dread so ill dissembled,
That in his hand the lightnings trembled.

Thy Godlike crime was to be kind,
To render with thy precepts less
The sum of human wretchedness,
And strengthen Man with his own mind;
But baffled as thou wert from high,
Still in thy patient energy,
In the endurance, and repulse
Of thine impenetrable Spirit,
Which Earth and Heaven could not convulse,
A mighty lesson we inherit:
Thou art a symbol and a sign
To Mortals of their fate and force;
Like thee, Man is in part divine,
A troubled stream from a pure source;
And Man in portions can foresee
His own funereal destiny;
His wretchedness, and his resistance,
And his sad unallied existence:
To which his Spirit may oppose
Itself - and equal to all woes,
And a firm will, and a deep sense,
Which even in torture can descry
Its own concenter'd recompense,
Triumphant where it dares defy,
And making Death a Victory.

"My Soul Is Dark"

My soul is dark - Oh! quickly string
The harp I yet can brook to hear;
And let thy gentle fingers fling
Its melting murmurs o'er mine ear.
If in this heart a hope be dear,
That sound shall charm it forth again:
If in these eyes there lurk a tear,
'Twill flow, and cease to burn my brain.
But bid the strain be wild and deep,
Nor let thy notes of joy be first:
I tell thee, minstrel, I must weep,
Or else this heavy heart will burst;
For it hath been by sorrow nursed,
And ached in sleepless silence, long;
And now 'tis doomed to know the worst,
And break at once - or yield to song.

PERCY BYSSHE SHELLEY
(1792-1822)

The Cloud

I bring fresh showers for the thirsting flowers,
    From the seas and the streams;
I bear light shade for the leaves when laid
    In their noonday dreams.
From my wings are shaken the dews that waken
    The sweet buds every one,
When rocked to rest on their mother's breast,
    As she dances about the sun,
I wield the flail of the lashing hail,
    And whiten the green plains under,
And then again I dissolve it in rain,
    And laugh as I pass in thunder.

I sift the snow on the mountains below,
    And their great pines groan aghast;
And all the night 'tis my pillow white,
    While I sleep in the arms of the blast.
Sublime on the towers of my skiey bowers,
    Lightning my pilot sits;
In a cavern under is fettered the thunder,
    It struggles and howls at fits;
Over earth and ocean, with gentle motion,
    This pilot is guiding me,
Lured by the love of the genii that move
    In the depths of the purple sea;
Over the rills, and the crags, and the hills,
    Over the lakes and the plains,
Wherever he dream, under mountain or stream,

The Spirit he loves remains;
And I all the while bask in Heaven's blue smile,
Whilst he is dissolving in rains.

The sanguine Sunrise, with his meteor eyes,
And his burning plumes outspread,
Leaps on the back of my sailing rack,
When the morning star shines dead;
As on the jag of a mountain crag,
Which an earthquake rocks and swings,
An eagle alit one moment may sit
In the light of its golden wings.
And when Sunset may breathe, from the lit sea beneath,
Its ardours of rest and of love,
And the crimson pall of eve may fall
From the depth of heaven above,
With wings folded I rest, on mine aëry nest,
As still as a brooding dove.

That orbèd maiden with white fire laden,
Whom mortals call the Moon,
Glides glimmering o'er my fleece-like floor,
By the midnight breezes strewn;
And wherever the beat of her unseen feet,
Which only the angels hear,
May have broken the woof of my tent's thin roof,
The stars peep behind her and peer;
And I laugh to see them whirl and flee,
Like a swarm of golden bees,
When I widen the rent in the wind-built tent,
Till the calm rivers,lakes, and seas,
Like strips of the sky fallen through me on high,
Are each paved with the moon and these.

I bind the Sun's throne with a burning zone,
       And the Moon's with a girdle of pearl;
The volcanoes are dim, and the stars reel and swim,
       When the whirlwinds my banner unfurl.
From cape to cape, with a bridge-like shape,
       Over the torrent sea,
Sunbeam-proof, I hang like a roof, –
       The mountains its column be.
The triumphal arch through which I march
       With hurricane, fire, and snow,
When the Powers of the air are chained to my chair,
       Is the million-coloured bow;
The sphere-fire above its soft colours wove,
       While the moist Earth was laughing below.

I am the daughter of Earth and Water,
       And the nursling of the Sky;
I pass through the pores of the ocean and shores;
       I change, but I cannot die.
For after the rain when with never a stain
       The pavilion of Heaven is bare,
And the winds and sunbeams with their convex gleams
       Build up the blue dome of air,
I silently laugh at my own cenotaph,
       And out of the caverns of rain,
Like a child from the womb, like a ghost from the tomb,
       I arise and unbuild it again.

Song

I

Rarely, rarely, comest thou,
   Spirit of Delight!
Wherefore hast thou left me now
   Many a day and night?
Many a weary night and day
'Tis since thou art fled away.

II

How shall ever one like me
   Win thee back again?
With the joyous and the free
   Thou wilt scoff at pain.
Spirit false! thou hadst forgot
   All but those who need thee not.

III

As a lizard with the shade
   Of a trembling leaf,
Thou with sorrow art dismayed;
   Even the sighs of grief
Reproach thee, that thou art not near,
And reproach thou wilt not hear.

IV

Let me set my mournful ditty
   To a merry measure;
Thou wilt never come for pity,
   Thou wilt come for pleasure;

Pity then ill cut away
Those cruel wings, and thou wilt stay.

V

I love all that thou lovest,
  Spirit of Delight!
The fresh Earth in new leaves dressed
  And the starry night;
Autumn evening, and the morn
When the golden mists are born.

VI

I love snow, and all the forms
  Of the radiant frost;
I love waves, and winds, and storms,
  Everything almost
Which is Nature's, and may be
Untainted by man's misery.

VII

I love tranquil solitude,
  And such society
As is quiet, wise, and good;
  Between thee and me
What difference? but thou dost possess
The things I seek, not love them less.

VIII

I love Love - though he has wings,
  And like light can flee,
But above all other things,

Spirit, I love thee –
Thou art love and life! Oh, come,
Make once more my heart thy home.

from *Adonais*

IX

Oh, weep for Adonais! – The quick Dreams,
The passion-wingèd Ministers of thought,
Who were his flocks, whom near the living streams
Of his young spirit he fed, and whom he taught
The love which was its music, wander not, –
Wander no more, from kindling brain to brain,
But droop there, whence they sprung; and mourn their lot
Round the cold heart, where, after their sweet pain,
They ne'er will gather strength, or find a home again.

XXVI

'Stay yet awhile! speak to me once again;
Kiss me, so long but as a kiss may live;
And in my heartless breast and burning brain
That word, that kiss, shall all thoughts else survive,
With food of saddest memory kept alive,
Now thou art dead, as if it were a part
Of thee, my Adonais! I would give
All that I am to be as thou now art!
But I am chained to Time, and cannot thence depart!

XXXIII

His head was bound with pansies overblown,
And faded violets, white, and pied, and blue;
And a light spear topped with a cypress cone,
Round whose rude shaft dark ivy-tresses grew
Yet dripping with the forest's noonday dew,
Vibrated, as the ever-beating heart

Shook the weak hand that grasped it; of that crew
He came the last, neglected and apart;
A herd-abandoned deer struck by the hunter's dart.

XLII

He is made one with Nature: there is heard
His voice in all her music, from the moan
Of thunder, to the song of night's sweet bird;
He is a presence to be felt and known
In darkness and in light, from herb and stone,
Spreading itself where'er that power may move
Which has withdrawn his being to its own;
Which wields the world with never-wearied love,
Sustains it from beneath, and kindles it above.

LII

The One remains, the many change and pass;
Heaven's light forever shines, Earth's shadows fly;
Life, like a dome of many-coloured glass,
Stains the white radiance of Eternity,
Until death tramples it to fragments. – Die,
If thou would'st be with that which thou dost seek!
Follow where all is fled! – Rome's azure sky,
Flowers, ruins, statues, music, words, are weak
The glory they transfuse with fitting truth to speak.

A Lament

I

O world! O life! O time!
On whose last steps I climb,
   Trembling at that where I had stood before;
When will return the glory of your prime?
       No more! Oh, nevermore!

II

Out of the day and night
A joy has taken flight;
   Fresh spring, and summer, and winter hoar,
Move my faint heart with grief, but with delight
       No more – Oh, never more!

Ozymandias

I met a traveller from an antique land
Who said: 'Two vast and trunkless legs of stone
Stand in the desert. Near them, on the sand,
Half sunk, a shattered visage lies, whose frown,
And wrinkled lip, and sneer of cold command,
Tell that its sculptor well those passions read
Which yet survive, stamped on these lifeless things,
The hand that mocked them and the heart that fed.
And on the pedestal these words appear –
"My name is Ozymandias, king of kings:
Look on my works, ye Mighty, and despair!"
Nothing beside remains. Round the decay
Of that colossal wreck, boundless and bare
The lone and level sands stretch far away.'

Mutability

We are the clouds that veil the midnight moon;
How restlessly they speed, and gleam, and quiver,
Streaking the darkness radiantly! – yet soon
Night closes round, and they are lost forever:

Or like forgotten lyres, whose dissonant strings
Give various response to each varying blast,
To whose frail frame no second motion brings
One mood or modulation like the last.

We rest. – A dream has power to poison sleep;
We rise. – One wandering thought pollutes the day;
We feel, conceive or reason, laugh or weep;
Embrace fond foe, or cast our cares away:

It is the same! – For, be it joy or sorrow,
The path of its departure still is free:
Man's yesterday may ne'er be like his morrow;
Nought may endure but Mutability.

Song of Prosperine

Sacred Goddess, Mother Earth,
Thou from whose immortal bosom
Gods and men and beasts have birth,
Leaf and blade, and bud and blossom,
Breathe thine influence most divine
On thine own child, Proserpine.

If with mists of evening dew
Thou dost nourish these young flowers
Till they grow in scent and hue
Fairest children of the Hours,
Breathe thine influence most divine
On thine own child, Proserpine.

Stanzas Written In Dejection Near Naples

The sun is warm, the sky is clear,
The waves are dancing fast and bright,
Blue isles and snowy mountains wear
The purple noon's transparent might,
The breath of the moist earth is light,
Around its unexpanded buds;
Like many a voice of one delight
The winds, the birds, the ocean floods,
The city's voice itself, is soft like Solitude's.

I see the deep's untrampled floor
With green and purple seaweeds strown;
I see the waves upon the shore,
Like light dissolved in star-showers, thrown:
I sit upon the sands alone, –
The lightning of the noontide ocean
Is flashing round me, and a tone
Arises from its measured motion,
How sweet! did any heart now share in my emotion.

Alas! I have nor hope nor health,
Nor peace within nor calm around,
Nor that content surpassing wealth
The sage in meditation found,
And walked with inward glory crowned –
Nor fame nor power, nor love, nor leisure,
Others I see whom these surround –
Smiling they live, and call life pleasure; –
To me that cup has been dealt in another measure.

Yet now despair itself is mild,
Even as the winds and waters are;
I could lie down like a tired child,
And weep away the life of care
Which I have born and yet must bear,
Till death like sleep might steal on me,
And I might feel in the warm air
My cheek grow cold, and hear the sea
Breathe o'er my dying brain its last monotony.

Some might lament that I were cold,
As I, when this sweet day is gone,
Which my lost heart, too soon grown old,
Insults with this untimely moan;
They might lament - for I am one
Whom men love not, - and yet regret,
Unlike this day, which, when the sun
Shall on its stainless glory set,
Will linger, though enjoyed, like joy in memory yet.

To Night

Swiftly walk o'er the western wave,
Spirit of Night!
Out of the misty eastern cave,
Where, all the long and lone daylight,
Thou wovest dreams of joy and fear,
Which make thee terrible and dear –
Swift be thy flight!

Wrap thy form in a mantle gray,
Star-inwrought!
Blind with thine hair the eyes of day;
Kiss her until she be wearied out,
Then wander o'er city, and sea, and land,
Touching all with thine opiate wand –
Come, long-sought!

When I arose and saw the dawn,
I sighed for thee;
When light rode high, and the dew was gone,
And noon lay heavy on flower and tree,
And the weary day turned to his rest,
Lingering like an unloved guest,
I sighed for thee.

Thy brother Death came, and cried,
Wouldst thou me?
Thy sweet child Sleep, the filmy-eyed,
Murmured like a noontide bee,
Shall I nestle near thy side?
Wouldst thou me? – And I replied,
No, not thee!

Death will come when thou art dead,
Soon, too soon –
Sleep will come when thou art fled;
Of neither would I ask the boon
I ask of thee, beloved Night –
Swift be thine approaching flight,
Come soon, soon!

FELICIA DOROTHEA HEMANS
(1793-1835)

The Rock of Cader Idris: A Legend of Wales

I lay on that rock where the storms have their dwelling,
The birthplace of phantom, the home of the cloud;
Around it for ever deep music is swelling,
The voice of the Mountain-wind, solemn and loud.
'Twas a midnight of shadows, all fitfully streaming,
Of wild gusts and torrents that mingled their moan,
Of dim-shrouded stars, as through gulfs faintly gleaming,
And my strife with stern nature was darksome and lone.

I lay there in silence: – a spirit came o'ver me;
Man's tongue hath no language to speak what I saw!
Things glorious, unearthly, passed floating before me,
And my heart almost fainted with rapture and awe!
I viewed the dread Beings around us that hover,
Though veiled by the mists of Mortality's breath;
And I called upon Darkness the vision to cover,
For within me was battling of madness and death!

I saw them – the Powers of the Wind and the Ocean,
The rush of whose pinion bears onward the storm;
Like the sweep of the white-rolling wave was their motion,
I felt their dread presence, but knew not their form.
I saw them – the mighty of ages departed –
The dead were around me that night on the hill;
From their eyes, as they passed, a cold radiance they darted;
There was light on my soul, but my heart's blood was chill.

I saw what man looks on, and dies! – but my spirit
Was strong, and triumphantly lived through that hour,
And as from the grave I awoke, to inherit
A flame all immortal, a voice and a power!
Day burst on that Rock with the purple cloud crested,
And high Cader Idris rejoiced in the sun;
But oh! what new glory all nature invested,
When the sense which gives *soul* to her beauty was won!

EMMA ROBERTS

(*c.* 1794-1840)

Night on the Ganges

How calm, how lovely is the soft repose
    Of nature sleeping in the summer night;
How sweet, how lullingly the current flows
    Beneath the stream of melted chrysolite,
Where Ganges spread its floods, – reflecting o'er
    Its silvery surface, with those countless stars
The ingot gems of heaven's cerulean floor,
    Mosques, groves, and cliffs, and pinnacled minarets.

The air is fresh, and yet the evening breeze
    Has died away; so hushed, 'tis scarcely heard
To breathe amid the clustering lemon trees,
    Whose snowy blossoms, by its faint sighs stirred,
Give out their perfume; and the bulbul's notes
    Awake the echoes of the balmy lime;
While from yon marble-domed pagoda float
    The music of its bell's soft, silvery chime.

Mildly, yet with resplendent beauty, shines
    The scene around, although the stars alone,
From the bright treasures of their gleaming mines
    A tender radiance o'er the earth have thrown.
Oh! far more lovely are those gentle rays
    With their undazzling lustre, than the beam
The sun pours down in his meridian blaze,
    Lighting with diamond pomp the sparkling stream.

Each tint its vivid colouring receives:
    There is the glossy peepul – the bamboo
Flings down its rich redundancy of leaves,
    And trailing plants their wandering course pursue,
In hues as bright as if the sun revealed
    The mantling foliage of the woody glade;
Nor is yon lone sequestered hut concealed
    Sleeping with the green hill's deepest shade.

With snowy vases crowned, the lily springs
    In queen-like beauty by the river's brink;
And o'er the wave the broad-leaved lotus flings
    Its roseate flowers in many a knotted link.
Oh! when the sultry sun has sunk to rest,
    When evening's soft and tender shadows rise,
How sweet the scene upon the river's breast,
    Beneath the starlight of these tropic skies!

JOHN CLARE
(1793-1864)

A Spring Morning

The spring comes in with all her hues and smells,
In freshness breathing over hills and dells;
O'er woods where May her gorgeous drapery flings,
And meads washed fragrant by their laughing springs.
Fresh are new opened flowers, untouched and free
From the bold rifling of the amorous bee,
The happy time of singing birds is come,
And Love's lone pilgrimage now finds a home;
Among the mossy oaks now coos the dove,
And the hoarse crow finds softer notes for love.
The foxes play around their dens, and bark
In joy's excess, 'mid woodland shadows dark.
The flowers join lips below; the leaves above;
And every sound that meets the ear is Love.

Love's Story

I do not love thee
So I'll not deceive thee.
I do love thee,
Yet I'm loth to leave thee.

I do not love thee
Yet joy's very essence
Comes with thy footstep,
Is complete in thy presence.

I do not love thee
Yet when gone, I sigh
And think about thee
Till the stars all die

I do not love thee
Yet thy bright black eyes
Bring to my heart's soul
Heaven and paradise

I do not love thee
Yet thy handsome ways
Bring me in absence
Almost hopeless days

I cannot hate thee
Yet my love seems debtor
To love thee more
So hating, love thee better.

To Mary

It is the evening hour,
  How silent all doth lie:
The hornèd moon she shows her face
  In the river with the sky.
Prest by the path on which we pass,
The flaggy lake lies still as glass.

Spirit of her I love,
  Whispering to me
Stores of sweet visions as I rove,
  Here stop, and crop with me
Sweet flowers that in the still hour grew –
We'll take them home, nor shake off the bright dew.

Mary, or sweet spirit of thee,
  As the bright sun shines tomorrow
Thy dark eyes these flowers shall seem
  Gathered by me in sorrow,
In the still hour when my mind was free
To walk alone – yet wish I walked with thee.

JOHN KEATS
(1795-1820)

Ode on Melancholy

I

No, no, go not to Lethe, neither twist
    Wolf's-bane, tight-rooted, for its poisonous wine;
Nor suffer thy pale forehead to be kiss'd
    By nightshade, ruby grape of Prosperine;
Make not your rosary of yew-berries,
    Nor let the beetle nor the death-moth be
        Your mournful Psyche, nor the downy owl
A partner in your sorrow's mysteries;
    For shade to shade will come too drowsily,
        And drown the wakeful anguish of the soul.

II

But when the melancholy fit shall fall
    Sudden from heaven like a weeping cloud,
That fosters the droop-headed flowers all,
    And hides the greenhill in an April shroud;
Then glut thy sorrow on a morning rose,
    Or on the rainbow of the salt sand-wave,
        Or on the wealth of globed peonies;
Or if thy mistress some rich anger shows,
    Emprison her soft hand, and let her rave,
        And feed deep, deep, upon her peerless eyes.

III

She dwells with beauty – Beauty that must die;
    And Joy, whose hand is ever at his lips
Bidding adieu; and aching Pleasure nigh,
    Turning to Poison while the bee-mouth sips:
Ay, in the very temple of Delight
    Veil'd Melancholy has her sovran shrine,
       Though seen of none save him whose strenuous tongue
    Can burst joy's grape against his palate fine:
His soul shall taste the sadness of her might,
       And be among her cloudy trophies hung.

"Bright star, would I were stedfast as thou art"

Bright star, would I were stedfast as thou art –
   Not in lone splendour hung aloft the night
And watching, with eternal lids apart,
   Like Nature's patient, sleepless Eremite,
The moving waters at their priestlike task
   Of pure ablution round earth's human shores,
Or gazing on the new soft-fallen mask
   Of snow upon the mountains and the moors –
No – yet still steadfast, still unchangeable,
   Pillow'd upon my fair love's ripening breast,
To feel for ever its soft fall and swell,
   Awake for ever in a sweet unrest,
Still, still to hear her tender-taken breath,
And so live ever – or else swoon to death.

La Belle Dame Sans Merci

I

O what can ail thee, knight-at-arms,
   Alone and palely loitering?
The sedge is wither'd from the lake,
   And no birds sing.

II

O what can ail thee, knight-at-arms,
   So haggard and so woe-begone?
The squirrel's granary is full,
   And the harvest's done.

III

I see a lily on thy brow
   With anguish moist and fever dew;
And on thy cheek a fading rose
   Fast withereth too.

IV

I met a lady in the meads,
   Full beautiful – a faery's child,
Her hair was long, her foot was light,
   And her eyes were wild.

V

I made a garland for her head,
   And bracelets too, and fragrant zone;
She look'd at me as she did love
   And made sweet moan.

VI

I set her on my pacing steed,
   And nothing else saw all day long,
For sideways would she lean, and sing
   A faery's song.

VII

She found me roots of relish sweet,
   And honey wild, and manna dew;
And sure in language strange she said –
   'I love thee true!'

VIII

She took me to her elfin grot,
   And there she gazed and sigh'd full sore,
And there I shut her wild wild eyes
   With kisses four.

IX

And there she lulled me asleep,
   And there I dream'd – ah! woe betide!\
The latest dream I ever dream'd
   On the cold hill side.

X

I saw pale kings and princes too,
    Pale warriors, death-pale were they all;
Who cried – 'La Belle Dame Sans Merci
    Hath thee in thrall!'

XI

I saw their starv'd lips in the gloam,
    With horrid warning gaped wide,
And I awoke, and found me here,
    On the cold hillside.

XII

And this is why I sojourn here,
    Alone and palely loitering,
Though the sedge is wither'd from the lake,
    And no birds sing.

Ode To a Nightingale

I

My heart aches, and a drowsy numbness pains
    My sense, as though of hemlock I had drunk,
Or emptied some dull opiate to the drains
    One minute past, and Lethe-wards had sunk:
'Tis not through envy of thy happy lot,
    But being too happy in thy happiness, –
        That thou, light-winged Dryad of the trees,
           In some melodious plot
    Of beechen green, and shadows numberless,
        Singes of summer in full-throated ease.

II

O for a draught of vintage! that hat been
    Cool'd a long age in the deep-delved earth,
Tasting of Flora and the country-green,
    Dance, and Provencal song, and sun-burnt mirth!
O for a beaker full of the warm South,
    Full of the true, the blushful Hippocrene,
        With beaded bubbles winking at the brim,
           And purple-stained mouth;
    That I might drink, and leave the world unseen,
        And with thee fade away into the forest dim:

III

Fade far away, dissolve, and quite forget
    What thou among the leaves hast never known,
The weariness, the fever, and the fret
    Here, where men sit and hear each other groan;
Where palsy shakes a few, sad, last gray hairs,
      Where youth grows pale, and spectre-thin, and dies;
        Where but to think is to be full of sorrow
          And leaden-eyed despairs;
      Where beauty cannot keep her lustrous eyes,
        Or new Love pine at them beyond to-morrow.

IV

Away! away! for I will fly to thee,
    Not charioted by bacchus and his pards,
But on the viewless wings of Poesy,
    Though the dull brain perplexes and retards:
Already with thee! tender is the night,
    And haply the Queen-Moon is on her throne,
      Clutter'd around by all her starry Fays;
        But here there is no light,
Save what from heaven is with the breezes blown
      Through verdurous glooms and winding mossy ways.

V

I cannot see what flowers are at my feet,
    Nor what soft incense hangs upon the boughs,
But, in embalmed darkness, guess each sweet
    Wherewith the seasonable month endows
The grass, the thicket, and the fruit-tree-wild;
    White hawthorn, and the pastoral eglantine;
      Fast-fading violets cover'd up in leaves;

And mid-May's eldest child,
The coming musk-rose, full of dewy-wine,
The murmurous haunt of flies on summer eves.

VI

Darkling I listen; and for many a time
I have been half in love with easeful Death,
Call'd him soft names in many a mused rhyme,
To take into the air my quiet breath;
Now more than ever seems it rich to die,
To cease upon the midnight with no pain,
While thou art pouring forth thy soul abroad
In such an ecstasy!
Still wouldst thou sing, and I have ears in vain –
To thy high requiem become a sod.

VII

Thou was not born for death, immortal Bird!
No hungry generations tread thee down;
The voice I hear this passing night was heard
In ancient days by emperor and clown:
Perhaps the self-same song that found a path
Through the sad heart of Ruth, when, sick for home,
She stood in tears amid the alien corn;
The same that oft-times hath
Charm'd magic casements, opening on the foam
Of perilous seas, in faery lands forlorn.

VIII

Forlorn! the very word is like a bell
To toll me back from thee to my sole grief!
Adieu! the fancy cannot cheat so well

As she is fam'd to do, deceiving elf.
Adieu! adieu! thy plaintive anthem fades
    Past the near meadows, over the still stream,
        Up the hill-side; and now 'tis buried deep
           In the next valley-glades:
    Was it a vision, or a waking dream?
        Fled is that music: – Do I wake or sleep?

To Solitude

O Solitude! if I must with thee dwell,
Let it not be among the jumbled heap
Of murky buildings; climb with me the steep, –
Nature's observatory – whence the dell,
Its flowery slopes, its river's crystal swell,
May seem a span; let me thy vigils keep
'Mongst boughs pavilion'd, where the deer's swift leap

Startles the wild bee from the foxglove bell.
But though I'll gladly trace these scenes with thee,
Yet the sweet converse of an innocent mind,
Whose words are images of thoughts refin'd,
Is my soul's pleasure; and it sure must be
Almost the highest bliss of human-kind,
When to thy haunts two kindred spirits flee.

The Eve of St Agnes

I

St. Agnes' Eve - Ah, bitter chill it was!
The owl, for all his feathers, was a-cold;
The hare limp'd trembling through the frozen grass,
And silent was the flock in woolly fold:
Numb were the Beadsman's fingers, while he told
His rosary, and while his frosted breath,
Like pious incense from a censer old,
Seem'd taking flight for heaven, without a death,
Past the sweet Virgin's picture, while his prayer he saith.

II

His prayer he saith, this patient, holy man;
Then takes his lamp, and riseth from his knees,
And back returneth, meagre, barefoot, wan,
Along the chapel aisle by slow degrees:
The sculptur'd dead, on each side, seem to freeze,
Emprison'd in black, purgatorial rails:
Knights, ladies, praying in dumb orat'ries,
He passeth by; and his weak spirit fails
To think how they may ache in icy hoods and mails.

III

Northward he turneth through a little door,
And scarce three steps, ere Music's golden tongue
Flatter'd to tears this aged man and poor;
But no - already had his deathbell rung
The joys of all his life were said and sung:

His was harsh penance on St. Agnes' Eve:
Another way he went, and soon among
Rough ashes sat he for his soul's reprieve,
And all night kept awake, for sinners' sake to grieve.

IV

That ancient Beadsman heard the prelude soft;
And so it chanc'd, for many a door was wide,
From hurry to and fro. Soon, up aloft,
The silver, snarling trumpets 'gan to chide:
The level chambers, ready with their pride,
Were glowing to receive a thousand guests:
The carved angels, ever eager-eyed,
Star'd, where upon their heads the cornice rests,
With hair blown back, and wings put cross-wise on
their breasts.

V

At length burst in the argent revelry,
With plume, tiara, and all rich array,
Numerous as shadows haunting fairily
The brain, new-stuff'd, in youth, with triumphs gay
Of old romance. These let us wish away,
And turn, sole-thoughted, to one lady there,
Whose heart had brooded, all that wintry day,
On love, and wing'd St Agnes' saintly care,
As she had heard old dames full rnany times declare.

VI

They told her how, upon St Agnes' Eve,
Young virgins might have visions of delight,
And soft adorings from their loves receive

Upon the honey'd middle of the night,
If ceremonies due they did aright;
As, supperless to bed they must retire,
And couch supine their beauties, lily white;
Nor look behind, nor sideways, but require
Of Heaven with upward eyes for all that they desire.

VII

Full of this whim was thoughtful Madeline:
The music, yearning like a God in pain,
She scarcely heard: her maiden eyes divine,
Fix'd on the floor, saw many a sweeping train
Pass by – she heeded not at all: in vain
Came many a tiptoe, amorous cavalier,
And back retir'd; not cool'd by high disdain,
But she saw not: her heart was otherwhere;
She sigh'd for Agnes' dreams, the sweetest of the year.

VIII

She danc'd along with vague, regardless eyes,
Anxious her lips, her breathing quick and short:
The hallow'd hour was near at hand: she sighs
Amid the timbrels, and the throng'd resort
Of whisperers in anger, or in sport;
'Mid looks of love, defiance, hate, and scorn,
Hoodwink'd with faery fancy; all amort,
Save to St Agnes and her lambs unshorn,
And all the bliss to be before to-morrow morn.

IX

So, purposing each moment to retire,
She linger'd still. Meantime, across the moors,
Had come young Porphyro, with heart on fire
For Madeline. Beside the portal doors,
Buttress'd from moonlight, stands he, and implores
All saints to give him sight of Madeline,
But for one moment in the tedious hours,
That he might gaze and worship all unseen;
Perchance speak, kneel, touch, kiss – in sooth such
                                things have been.

X

He ventures in: let no buzz'd whisper tell:
All eyes be muffled, or a hundred swords
Will storm his heart, Love's fev'rous citadel:
For him, those chambers held barbarian hordes,
Hyena foemen, and hot-blooded lords,
Whose very dogs would execrations howl
Against his lineage: not one breast affords
Him any mercy, in that mansion foul,
Save one old beldame, weak in body and in soul.

XI

Ah, happy chance! the aged creature came,
Shuffling along with ivory-headed wand,
To where he stood, hid from the torch's flame,
Behind a broad hall-pillar, far beyond
The sound of merriment and chorus bland.
He startled her; but soon she knew his face,
And grasp'd his fingers in her palsied hand,
Saying, "Mercy, Porphyro! hie thee from this place;

"They are all here to-night, the whole blood-thirsty race!

XII

    "Get hence! get hence! there's dwarfish Hildebrand;
He had a fever late, and in the fit
He cursed thee and thine, both house and land:
Then there's that old Lord Maurice, not a whit
More tame for his gray hairs - Alas me! flit!
Flit like a ghost away." - "Ah, gossip dear,
We're safe enough; here in this arm-chair sit,
And tell me how" - "Good saints! not here, not here;
Follow me, child, or else these stones will be thy bier."

XIII

    He follow'd through a lowly arched way,
Brushing the cobwebs with his lofty plume,
And as she mutter'd "Well-a - well-a-day!"
He found him in a little moonlight room,
Pale, lattic'd, chill, and silent as a tomb.
"Now tell me where is Madeline", said he,
"O tell me, Angela, by the holy loom
Which none but secret sisterhood may see,
"When they St Agnes' wool are weaving piously."

XIV

    "St Agnes! Ah! it is St Agnes' Eve -
Yet men will murder upon holy days:
Thou must hold water in a witch's sieve,
And be liege-lord of all the Elves and Fays
To venture so: it fills me with amaze
To see thee, Porphyro! - St Agnes' Eve!
God's help! my lady fair the conjuror plays

This very night: good angels her deceive!
But let me laugh awhile, I've mickle time to grieve."

XV

Feebly she laugheth in the languid moon,
While Porphyro upon her face doth look,
Like puzzled urchin on an aged crone
Who keepeth clos'd a wondrous riddle-book,
As spectacled she sits in chimney nook.
But soon his eyes grew brilliant, when she told
His lady's purpose; and he scarce could brook
Tears, at the thought of those enchantments cold
And Madeline asleep in lap of legends old.

XVI

Sudden a thought came like a full-blown rose,
Flushing his brow, and in his pained heart
Made purple riot: then doth he propose
A stratagem, that makes the beldame start:
"A cruel man and impious thou art:
Sweet lady, let her pray, and sleep, and dream
Alone with her good angels, far apart
From wicked men like thee. Go, go! – I deem
Thou canst not surely be the same that thou didst seem."

XVII

"I will not harm her, by all saints I swear,"
Quoth Porphyro: "O may I ne'er find grace
When my weak voice shall whisper its last prayer,
If one of her soft ringlets I displace,
Or look with ruffian passion in her face:
Good Angela, believe me by these tears;

Or I will, even in a moment's space,
    Awake, with horrid shout, my foemen's ears,
And beard them, though they be more fang'd than
                wolves and bears."

XVIII

    "Ah! why wilt thou affright a feeble soul?
    A poor, weak, palsy-stricken, churchyard thing,
    Whose passing-bell may ere the midnight toll;
    Whose prayers for thee, each morn and evening,
    Were never miss'd." Thus plaining, doth she bring
    A gentler speech from burning Porphyro;
    So woeful, and of such deep sorrowing,
    That Angela gives promise she will do
Whatever he shall wish, betide her weal or woe.

XIX

    Which was, to lead him, in close secrecy,
    Even to Madeline's chamber, and there hide
    Him in a closet, of such privacy
    That he might see her beauty unespied,
    And win perhaps that night a peerless bride,
    While legion'd fairies pac'd the coverlet,
    And pale enchantment held her sleepy-eyed.
    Never on such a night have lovers met,
Since Merlin paid his Demon all the monstrous debt.

XX

    "It shall be as thou wishest," said the Dame:
    "All cates and dainties shall be stored there
    Quickly on this feast-night: by the tambour frame
    Her own lute thou wilt see: no time to spare,

For I am slow and feeble, and scarce dare
On such a catering trust my dizzy head.
Wait here, my child, with patience; kneel in prayer
The while: Ah! thou must needs the lady wed,
Or may I never leave my grave among the dead."

XXI

So saying, she hobbled off with busy fear.
The lover's endless minutes slowly pass'd;
The Dame return'd, and whisper'd in his ear
To follow her; with aged eyes aghast
From fright of dim espial. Safe at last
Through many a dusky gallery, they gain
The maiden's chamber, silken, hush'd and chaste;
Where Porphyro took covert, pleas'd amain.
His poor guide hurried back with agues in her brain.

XXII

Her falt'ring hand upon the balustrade,
Old Angela was feeling for the stair,
When Madeline, St Agnes' charmed maid,
Rose, like a mission'd spirit, unaware:
With silver taper's light, and pious care,
She turn'd, and down the aged gossip led
To a safe level matting. Now prepare,
Young Porphyro, for gazing on that bed;
She comes, she comes again, like dove fray'd and fled.

XXIII

Out went the taper as she hurried in;
Its little smoke, in pallid moonshine, died:
She closed the door, she panted, all akin

To spirits of the air, and visions wide:
No utter'd syllable, or, woe betide!
But to her heart, her heart was voluble,
Paining with eloquence her balmy side;
As though a tongueless nightingale should swell
Her throat in vain, and die, heart-stifled, in her dell.

XXIV

A casement high and triple-arch'd there was,
All garlanded with carven imag'ries
Of fruits, and flowers, and bunches of knot-grass,
And diamonded with panes of quaint device,
Innumerable of stains and splendid dyes,
As are the tiger-moth's deep-damask'd wings;
And in the midst, 'mong thousand heraldries,
And twilight saints, and dim emblazonings,
A shielded scutcheon blush'd with blood of queens and kings.

XXV

Full on this casement shone the wintry moon,
And threw warm gules on Madeline's fair breast,
As down she knelt for heaven's grace and boon;
Rose-bloom fell on her hands, together prest,
And on her silver cross soft amethyst,
And on her hair a glory, like a saint:
She seem'd a splendid angel, newly drest,
Save wings, for heaven: – Porphyro grew faint:
She knelt, so pure a thing, so free from mortal taint.

XXVI

Anon his heart revives: her vespers done,
Of all its wreathed pearls her hair she frees;
Unclasps her warmed jewels one by one;
Loosens her fragrant bodice; by degrees
Her rich attire creeps rustling to her knees:
Half-hidden, like a mermaid in sea-weed,
Pensive awhile she dreams awake, and sees,
In fancy, fair St Agnes in her bed,
But dares not look behind, or all the charm is fled.

XXVII

Soon, trembling in her soft and chilly nest,
In sort of wakeful swoon, perplex'd she lay,
Until the poppied warmth of sleep oppress'd
Her soothed limbs, and soul fatigued away;
Flown, like a thought, until the morrow-day;
Blissfully haven'd both from joy and pain;
Clasp'd like a missal where swart Paynims pray;
Blinded alike from sunshine and from rain,
As though a rose should shut, and be a bud again.

XXVIII

Stol'n to this paradise, and so entranced,
Porphyro gazed upon her empty dress,
And listen'd to her breathing, if it chanced
To wake into a slumbrous tenderness;
Which when he heard, that minute did he bless,
And breath'd himself: then from the closet crept,
Noiseless as fear in a wide wilderness,
And over the hush'd carpet, silent, stept,

And 'tween the curtains peep'd, where, lo! – how fast
                                                    she slept!

XXIX

    Then by the bed-side, where the faded moon
    Made a dim, silver twilight, soft he set
    A table, and, half anguish'd, threw thereon
    A doth of woven crimson, gold, and jet: –
    O for some drowsy Morphean amulet!
    The boisterous, midnight, festive clarion,
    The kettle-drum, and far-heard clarinet,
    Affray his ears, though but in dying tone: –
The hall door shuts again, and all the noise is gone.

XXX

    And still she slept an azure-lidded sleep,
    In blanched linen, smooth, and lavender'd,
    While he from forth the closet brought a heap
    Of candied apple, quince, and plum, and gourd
    With jellies soother than the creamy curd,
    And lucent syrops, tinct with cinnamon;
    Manna and dates, in argosy transferr'd
    From Fez; and spiced dainties, every one,
From silken Samarcand to cedar'd Lebanon.

XXXI

    These delicates he heap'd with glowing hand
    On golden dishes and in baskets bright
    Of wreathed silver: sumptuous they stand
    In the retired quiet of the night,
    Filling the chilly room with perfume light. –
    "And now, my love, my seraph fair, awake!

Thou art my heaven, and I thine eremite:
Open thine eyes, for meek St Agnes' sake,
Or I shall drowse beside thee, so my soul doth ache."

XXXII

Thus whispering, his warm, unnerved arm
Sank in her pillow. Shaded was her dream
By the dusk curtains: - 'twas a midnight charm
Impossible to melt as iced stream:
The lustrous salvers in the moonlight gleam;
Broad golden fringe upon the carpet lies:
It seem'd he never, never could redeem
From such a stedfast spell his lady's eyes;
So mus'd awhile, entoil'd in woofed phantasies.

XXXIII

Awakening up, he took her hollow lute, -
Tumultuous, - and, in chords that tenderest be,
He play'd an ancient ditty, long since mute,
In Provence call'd, "La belle dame sans mercy:"
Close to her ear touching the melody: -
Wherewith disturb'd, she utter'd a soft moan:
He ceased - she panted quick - and suddenly
Her blue affrayed eyes wide open shone:
Upon his knees he sank, pale as smooth-sculptured stone.

XXXIV

Her eyes were open, but she still beheld,
Now wide awake, the vision of her sleep:
There was a painful change, that nigh expell'd
The blisses of her dream so pure and deep,
At which fair Madeline began to weep,

And moan forth witless words with many a sigh;
While still her gaze on Porphyro would keep;
Who knelt, with joined hands and piteous eye,
Fearing to move or speak, she look'd so dreamingly.

XXXV

"Ah, Porphyro!" said she, "but even now
Thy voice was at sweet tremble in mine ear,
Made tuneable with every sweetest vow;
And those sad eyes were spiritual and clear:
How chang'd thou art! how pallid, chill, and drear!
Give me that voice again, my Porphyro,
Those looks immortal, those complainings dear!
Oh leave me not in this eternal woe,
For if thou diest, my Love, I know not where to go."

XXXVI

Beyond a mortal man impassion'd far
At these voluptuous accents, he arose,
Ethereal, flush'd, and like a throbbing star
Seen mid the sapphire heaven's deep repose
Into her dream he melted, as the rose
Blendeth its odour with the violet, –
Solution sweet: meantime the frost-wind blows
Like Love's alarum pattering the sharp sleet
Against the window-panes; St Agnes' moon hath set.

XXXVII

Tis dark: quick pattereth the flaw-blown sleet:
"This is no dream, my bride, my Madeline!"
'Tis dark: the iced gusts still rave and beat:
"No dream, alas! alas! and woe is mine!

Porphyro will leave me here to fade and pine. –
Cruel! what traitor could thee hither bring?
I curse not, for my heart is lost in thine
Though thou forsakest a deceived thing; –
A dove forlorn and lost with sick unpruned wing."

XXXVIII

"My Madeline! sweet dreamer! lovely bride!
Say, may I be for aye thy vassal blest?
Thy beauty's shield, heart-shap'd and vermeil dyed?
Ah, silver shrine, here will I take my rest
After so many hours of toil and quest,
A famish'd pilgrim, – saved by miracle.
Though I have found, I will not rob thy nest
Saving of thy sweet self; if thou think'st well
To trust, fair Madeline, to no rude infidel.

XXXIX

"Hark! 'tis an elfin-storm from faery land,
Of haggard seeming, but a boon indeed:
Arise – arise! the morning is at hand; –
The bloated wassailers will never heed: –
Let us away, my love, with happy speed;
There are no ears to hear, or eyes to see, –
Drown'd all in Rhenish and the sleepy mead:
Awake! arise! my love, and fearless be,
For o'er the southern moors I have a home for thee."

XL

She hurried at his words, beset with fears,
For there were sleeping dragons all around,
At glaring watch, perhaps, with ready spears –

Down the wide stairs a darkling way they found. –
In all the house was heard no human sound.
A chain-droop'd lamp was flickering by each door;
The arras, rich with horseman, hawk, and hound,
Flutter'd in the besieging wind's uproar;
And the long carpets rose along the gusty floor.

XLI

They glide, like phantoms, into the wide hall;
Like phantoms, to the iron porch, they glide;
Where lay the Porter, in uneasy sprawl,
With a huge empty flagon by his side:
The wakeful bloodhound rose, and shook his hide,
But his sagacious eye an inmate owns:
By one, and one, the bolts fill easy slide: –
The chains lie silent on the footworn stones, –
The key turns, and the door upon its hinges groans.

XLII

And they are gone: ay, ages long ago
These lovers fled away into the storm.
That night the Baron dreamt of many a woe,
And all his warrior-guests, with shade and form
Of witch, and demon, and large coffin-worm,
Were long be-nightmar'd. Angela the old
Died palsy-twitch'd, with meagre face deform;
The Beadsman, after thousand aves told,
For aye unsought for slept among his ashes cold.

ELIZABETH BARRETT BROWNING
(1806-1861)

from *Sonnets From the Portuguese*

XXI

Say over again, and yet once over again,
That thou dost love me. Though the word repeated
Should seem 'a cuckoo-song,' as thou dost treat it.
Remember, never to the hill or plain,
Valley and wood, without her cuckoo-strain
Comes the fresh Spring in all her green completed.
Belovèd, I, amid the darkness greeted
By a doubtful spirit-voice, in that doubt's pain
Cry… 'Speak once more… thou lovest!' Who can fear
Too many stars, though each in heaven shall roll, –
Too many flowers, though each shall crown the year?
Say thou love me, love me, love me – toll
The silver iterance! – only minding, Dear,
To love me also in silence with thy soul.

XXII

When our two souls stand up erect and strong,
Face to face, silent, drawing nigh and nigher,
Until the lengthening wings break into fire
At either curvèd point, – what bitter wrong
Can the earth do to us, that we should not long
Be here contented? Think. In mourning higher,
The angels would press on us and aspire
To drop some golden orb of perfect song
Into our deep, dear silence. Let us stay
Rather on earth, Belovèd, – where the unfit
Contrarious moods of men recoil away
And isolate pure spirits, and permit
A place to stand and love in for a day,
With darkness and the death-hour rounding it.

MARY WOLLSTONECRAFT SHELLEY
(1797-1851)

Stanzas

Oh, come to me in dreams, my love!
   I will not ask a dearer bliss;
Come with the starry beams, my love,
   And press mine eyelids with thy kiss.

'Twas thus, as ancient fables tell,
   Love visited a Grecian maid,
Till she disturbed the sacred spell,
   And woke to find her hopes betrayed.

But gentle sleep shall veil my sight,
   And Psyche's lamp shall darkling be.
When, in the visions of the night,
   Thou dost renew thy vows to me.

Then come to me in dreams, my love,
   I will not ask a dearer bliss:
Come with the starry beams, my love,
   And press mine eyelids with thy kiss.

EDGAR ALLAN POE
(1809-1849)

A Dream

In visions of the dark night
I have dreamed of joy departed
But a waking dream of life and light
Hath left me broken-hearted.

Ah! what is not a dream by day
To him whose eyes are cast
On things around him with a ray
Turned back upon the past?

That holy dream – that holy dream,
While all the world were chiding,
Hath cheered me as a lovely beam
A lonely spirit guiding.

What though that light, thro' storm and night,
So trembled from afar
What could there be more purely bright
In Truth's day-star?

The Bells

I

Hear the sledges with the bells
Silver bells!
What a world of merriment their melody foretells!
How they tinkle, tinkle, tinkle,
In the icy air of night!
While the stars that oversprinkle
All the heavens, seem to twinkle
With a crystalline delight;
Keeping time, time, time,
In a sort of Runic rhyme,
To the tintinnabulation that so musically wells
From the bells, bells, bells, bells,
Bells, bells, bells
From the jingling and the tinkling of the bells.

II

Hear the mellow wedding bells,
Golden bells!
What a world of happiness their harmony foretells!
Through the balmy air of night
How they ring out their delight!
From the molten-golden notes,
And an in tune,
What a liquid ditty floats
To the turtle-dove that listens, while she gloats
On the moon!
Oh, from out the sounding cells,
What a gush of euphony voluminously wells!

How it swells!
How it dwells
On the Future! how it tells
Of the rapture that impels
To the swinging and the ringing
Of the bells, bells, bells,
Of the bells, bells, bells,bells,
Bells, bells, bells
To the rhyming and the chiming of the bells!

III

Hear the loud alarum bells
Brazen bells!
What a tale of terror, now, their turbulency tells!
In the startled ear of night
How they scream out their affright!
Too much horrified to speak,
They can only shriek, shriek,
Out of tune,
In a clamorous appealing to the mercy of the fire,
In a mad expostulation with the deaf and frantic fire,
Leaping higher, higher, higher,
With a desperate desire,
And a resolute endeavor,
Now - now to sit or never,
By the side of the pale-faced moon.

Oh, the bells, bells, bells!
What a tale their terror tells
Of Despair!
How they clang, and clash, and roar!
What a horror they outpour
On the bosom of the palpitating air!

Yet the ear it fully knows,
By the twanging,
And the clanging,
How the danger ebbs and flows:
Yet the ear distinctly tells,
In the jangling,
And the wrangling,
How the danger sinks and swells,
By the sinking or the swelling in the anger of the bells
Of the bells
Of the bells, bells, bells,bells,
Bells, bells, bells
In the clamor and the clangor of the bells!

IV

Hear the tolling of the bells
Iron Bells!
What a world of solemn thought their monody compels!
In the silence of the night,
How we shiver with affright
At the melancholy menace of their tone!
For every sound that floats
From the rust within their throats
Is a groan.
And the people – ah, the people
They that dwell up in the steeple,
All Alone
And who, tolling, tolling, tolling,
In that muffled monotone,
Feel a glory in so rolling
On the human heart a stone
They are neither man nor woman
They are neither brute nor human

They are Ghouls:
And their king it is who tolls;
And he rolls, rolls, rolls,
Rolls
A paean from the bells!
And his merry bosom swells
With the paean of the bells!
And he dances, and he yells;
Keeping time, time, time,
In a sort of Runic rhyme,
To the paean of the bells
Of the bells:
Keeping time, time, time,
In a sort of Runic rhyme,
To the throbbing of the bells
Of the bells, bells, bells
To the sobbing of the bells;
Keeping time, time, time,
As he knells, knells, knells,
In a happy Runic rhyme,
To the rolling of the bells
Of the bells, bells, bells:
To the tolling of the bells,
Of the bells, bells, bells, bells
Bells, bells, bells
To the moaning and the groaning of the bells.

CHARLOTTE BRONTE
(1816-1855)

"What does she dream of, lingering all alone"

What does she dream of, lingering alone
   On the vast terrace, o'er that stream impending?
Through all the dim, still night no life-like tone
   With the soft rush of wind and wave is blending.
Her fairy step upon the marble falls
With startling echo through those silent halls.

Chill is the night, though glorious, and she folds
   Her robe upon her breast to meet that blast
Coming down from the barren Northern wolds.
   There, how she shuddered as the breeze blew past
And died on yonder track of foam, with shiver
Of giant reed and flag fringing the river.

Full, brilliant shines the moon – lifted on high
   O'er noble land and nobler river flowing,
Through parting hills that swell upon that sky
   Still with the hue of dying daylight glowing,
Swell with their plumy woods and dewy glades,
Opening to moonlight in the deepest shades.

Turn lady to thy halls, for singing shrill
   Again the gust descends – again the river
Frets into foam – I see thy dark eyes fill
   With large and bitter tears – thy sweet lips quiver.

EMILY BRONTE

(1818-1848)

"That wind, I used to hear it swelling"

That wind, I used to hear it swelling
With joy divinely deep;
You might have seen my hot tears welling,
But rapture made me weep.

I used to love on winter nights
To lie and dream alone
Of all the rare and real delights
My early years had known;

And oh, above the rest of those
That coming time should bear,
Like heaven's own glorious stars they rose
Still beaming bright and fair.

"Loud without the wind was roaring"

Loud without the wind was roaring
Through the waned autumnal sky;
Drenching wet, the cold rain pouring
Spoke of stormy winters nigh.

All too like that dreary eve
Sighed within repining grief;
Sighed at first, but sighed not long –
Sweet – How softly sweet it came!
Wild words of an ancient song,
Undefined, without a name.

"It was spring, for the skylark was singing."
Those words, they awakened a spell –
They unlocked a deep fountain whose springing
Nor Absence nor Distance can quell.

In the gloom of a cloudy November,
They uttered the music of May;
They kindled the perishing ember
Into fervour that could not decay.

Awaken on all my dear moorlands
The wind in its glory and pride!
O call me from valleys and highlands
To walk by the hill-river's side!

It is swelled with the first snowy weather;
The rocks they are icy and hoar
And darker waves round the long heather
And the fern-leaves are sunny no more,

There are no yellow-stars on the mountain,
The blue-bells have long died away
From the brink of the moss-bedded fountain,
From the side of the wintery brae –

But lovelier than corn-fields allow having
In emerald and scarlet and gold
Are the slopes where the north-wind is raving,
And the glens where I wandered of old.

"It was morning; the bright sun was beaming.'
How sweetly that brought back to me
The time when nor labour nor dreaming
Broke the sleep of the happy and the free.

But blindly we rose as the dusk heaven
Was melting to amber and blue;
And swift were the wings to our feet given
While we traversed the meadows of dew.

For the moors, for the moors where the short grass
Like velvet beneath us should lie!
For the moors, for the moors where each high pass
Rose sunny against the clear sky!

For the moors where the linnet was trilling
Its song on the old granite stone;
Where the lark – the wild skylark was filling
Every breast with delight like its own.

What language can utter the feeling
That rose when, in exile afar,
On the brow of a lonely hill kneeling
I saw the brown heath growing there.

It was scattered and stunted, and told me
That soon even that would be gone;
Its whispered, "The grim walls enfold me;
I have bloomed in my last summer's sun."

But not the loved music whose waking
Makes the soul of the Swiss die away
Has a spell more adored and heart-breaking
Than in its half blighted bells lay.

The spirit that bent 'neath its power,
How it longed, how it burned to be free!
If I could have wept in that hour
Those tears had been heaven to me.

Well, well, the sad minutes are moving
Though loaded with trouble and pain;
And sometime the loved and the loving
Shall meet on the mountains again.

"High waving heather, 'neath stormy blasts bending"

High waving heather, 'neath stormy blasts bending,
Midnight and moonlight and bright shining stars;
Darkness and glory rejoicingly blending,
Earth rising to heaven and heaven descending,
Man's spirit away from its drear dungeon sending,
Bursting the fetters and breaking the bars.

All down the mountain sides, wild forests lending
One might voice to the life-giving wind;
Rivers their banks in the jubilee rending,
Fast through the valleys a reckless course wending,
Wider and deeper their waters extending,
Leaving a desolate desert behind.

Shining and lowering and swelling and dying,
Changing for ever from midnight to noon;
Roaring like thunder, like soft music sighing,
Shadows on shadows advancing and flying,
Lightning-bright flashes the deep gloom defying,
Coming as swiftly and fading as soon.

Stars

Ah! why, because the dazzling sun
Restored our Earth to joy,
Have you departed, every one,
And left a desert sky?

All through the night, your glorious eyes
Were gazing down in mine,
And, with a full heart's thankful sighs,
I blessed that watch divine.

I was at peace, and drank your beams
As they were life to me;
And revelled in my changeful dreams,
Like petrel on the sea.

Thought followed thought, star followed star
Through boundless regions on;
While one sweet influence, near and far,
Thrilled through, and proved us one!

Why did the morning dawn to break
So great, so pure a spell;
And scorch with fire the tranquil cheek,
Where your cool radiance fell?

Blood-red, he rose, and arrow-straight,
His fierce beams struck my brow;
The soul of nature sprang, elate,
But mine sank sad and low.

My lids closed down, yet through their veil
I saw him, blazinig, still,

And steep in gold the misty dale,
And flash upon the hill.

I turned me to the pillow, then,
To call back night, and see
Your words of solemn light, again,
Throb with my heart, and me!

It would not do - the pillow glowed,
And glowed both roof and floor;
And birds sang loudly in the wood,
And fresh winds shook the door;

The curtains waved, the wakened flies
Were murmuring round my room,
Imprisoned there, till I should rise,
And give them leave to roam.

O stars, and dreams, and gentle night;
O night and stars, return!
And hide me from the hostile light
That does not warm, but burn;

That drains the blood of suffering men;
Drinks tears, instead of dew;
Let me sleep through his blinding reign,
And only wake with you!

"Mild the mist upon the hill"

Mild the mist upon the hill,
Telling not of stones tomorrow;
No; the day has wept its fill,
Spent its store of silent sorrow.

Oh, I'm gone back to the days of youth,
I am a child once more;
And 'neath my father's sheltering roof,
And near the old hall door,

I watch this cloudy evening fall,
After a day of rain:
Blue mists, sweet mists of summer pall
The horizon's mountain-chain.

The damp stands in the long, green grass
As thick as morning's tears;
And dreamy scents of fragrance pass
That breathe of other years.

GALLERY OF POETS

Thomas Phillips, William Blake

Mary Robinson, Thomas Gainsborough, 1781, Wallace Collection, London

William Wordsworth, 1842, National Portrait Gallery, London

Lord Byron, 1814

Samuel Taylor Coleridge

John Clare, by William Hilton, 1820, National Portrait Gallery, London

Percy Bysshe Shelley

John Keats

Elizabeth Barrett Browning, by Macaire Havre,1859.

The Brontë sisters, by their brother Bramwell, c. 1834

Edgar Allan Poe, 1898

Richard Rothwell, Portrait of Mary Shelley, 1840

A NOTE ON
ENGLISH ROMANTIC POETRY

Among all the British Romantic poets, John Keats was perhaps the most typical: he exalted pagan imagery; he employed much ancient Greek and Roman mythology; he was a shamanic poet, who wrote in feverish bouts; he was a 'Muse poet'; he wrote searing short poems, and attempted long, 'epic' sequences; he revered the right authors (Milton, Shakespeare, the ancient Greeks); he travelled to Italy, *the* destination for the authentic Grand Tour experience; and he died young. John Keats was one of the few British poets who was truly ecstatic and wild. Despite the overly-ornate language, the often clumsy phrases, despite the Romantic indulgences and the sexist views, despite often over-simplification of natural and human processes and experiences, despite the tendency to gush and exaggerate, Keats was one of the few British poets who was truly shamanic. He was the British poet closest to the pure intoxication of Arthur Rimbaud. Keats reached the pinnacle of British poetry, as W. Jackson Bate, typical among critics, said: 'the language of his greatest poetry has always held a magnetic attraction; for there we reach, if only for a brief while, a high plateau where in mastery of phrase he has few equals in English poetry, and only one obvious superior.'[1]

Like Rimbaud, and like the poet he is most compared with, Shelley, Keats burnt fiercely and died young. He is a poet as martyr and hero, a Vincent van Gogh of poesie. He is famous for his sensual odes, 'Ode to a Grecian Urn', 'Ode to Melancholy', 'To Autumn', 'Ode to Psyche' and 'Ode to a Nightingale', the longer poems *Lamia*, *Endymion* and *Hyperion*, the luxuriant 'The Eve of St Agnes', a group of sonnets and the strange, haunting poem 'La Belle Dame Sans Merci'.

John Keats' sensualism is critically acclaimed. His poetry abounds in sensual experiences. Not just the visual and aural, but also, especially, of touch and taste, and smell. The effect is, as with Rimbaud or Coleridge, synæsthetic. Coleridge wrote of being amidst Nature in a similar way to Keats. In this extract from Coleridge's letters, one can also see aspects of the eternal breath or wind which Shelley so loved:

> In simple earnest, I never find myself alone within the embracement of rocks and hills, a traveller up an alpine road, but my spirit courses, drives, and eddies, like a heat in Autumn: a wild activity, of thoughts, imagination, feelings, and impulses of motion, rises up from within me – a sort of *bottom-wind*, that blows to no point of the compass, and comes from I know not whence, but agitates the whole of me...[2]

The Romantic poets wrote some of the greatest Nature poetry in literature, as the poems collected here demonstrate. Coleridge's poetry was very sensitive to weather; his repressions would either result in rheumatism or poetry. 'Dejection' can be seen a poetic record of depression brought on by bad weather: it 'must be the most famous analysis of pre-storm weather ever written' said Peter Redgrove.[3] Much of Byron's *Childe Harold* was concerned with lyrical descriptions of exotic landscapes. The elemental powers of Nature are very much to the fore in poems such as William Cowper's 'To the Nightingale', Charlotte Smith's 'To the South Downs' and 'Beachy Head', William Blake's 'Night', Mary

Robinson's 'Written After Successive Nights of Melancholy Dream', Helen Maria Williams's 'Sonnet: To the Torrid Zone', Dorothy Wordsworth's 'Floating Island at Hawkshead', Felicia Dorothea Hemans' 'The Rock of Cader Idris', Emma Roberts' 'Night on the Ganges', Barbara Hoole's Ullswater sonnet, much of the poetry of John Clare and Emily Brontë, and of course the king of Romantic Nature poetry, William Wordsworth (in poems such as 'Lines Composed a Few Miles Above Tintern Abbey', 'Ode: Intimations of Immortality', 'I Wandered Lonely As a Cloud' and *The Prelude*).

In Shelley's poetry, as in so much of Romantic poetry, Nature is idealized and idealism is treated in a naturalistic fashion. For the poet, there is not necessarily a conflict between ideas and actualities, between dreams and waking experiences, or between art and life. In poems such as 'The Cloud', 'Ode to the West Wind' and 'To a Skylark', Shelley demonstrated a delicate and detailed grasp of meteorology, and the poetry of weather. When it comes to nature poetry and nature mysticism, Shelley turns out to be as successful as that god of English pantheism, Wordsworth. Throughout Shelley's poetry the force of Nature rages. At times, all he does is to conjure up scenes, or to list effects and visions, just like Keats in 'The Eve of St Agnes' or Wordsworth in *The Prelude*. Nature poetry can read as a series of linguistic fireworks, without much substance. One can see Henry Vaughan, Shakespeare, Novalis, Goethe and Wordsworth as producers of lists of natural effects. Taken out of the context of the lengthy pieces such as *Prometheus Unbound, The Revolt of Islam* or *Queen Mab*, Shelley's nature poetry bears up well to detailed analysis, as well as consumption simply for entertainment. 'Poetry is ever accompanied with pleasure' Shelley writes in *A Defence of Poetry* (*Selected Poetry and Prose*, 210).

Art must entertain as well enrich or enlighten, and Shelley, like Keats or Coleridge, is certainly entertaining. He is full of exuberantly described images of rivers, forests, suns, cities, mænads and deities. Shelley might be over-lush for some tastes. Certainly he is as rich a poet, in terms of sensual imagery, as there is. Certainly, too, he is in love with his ability to create word-pictures. He is self-conscious about his word magic. He knows what he is doing with his poetic effects. At times Shelley is all too delicate, all too self-consciously elegant. Many of his lines end, like those of many Romantic poets, with an exclamation mark. He writes, so often, in a state of great excitement: 'clasped my hands in ecstasy!' ('Hymn to Intellectual Beauty'), '[p]aradise of golden lights!' ('Ode to Heaven'), '[v]oice the sweetest ever heard!' ('To Mary ---'), 'thou shouldst now depart!' ('Adonais').

For Catherine Belsey, Shelley's poetry is typical of Romantic poetry, because it is, ultimately, about its own making, rather than 'about' clouds or gods or love or emotions. It is a poetry that is a sophisticated mirror. Belsey writes:

> In the Romantic ode poetry enshrines the record of its own birth. The account of the vision is the poem itself and therefore it is the poem which constitutes the proof of the validity of the vision, the truth of the intimations of immortality which the text records. The poem then generates in the reader a participation in these intimations, and this is the source of its power to transcend and transform the world, to redeem it from death. In Shelley's version the West Wind symbolizes both the poetic vision which is to bring life to the poet and the 'incantation' of the poem itself which will 'quicken a new birth' in the dying world. The poem is thus a perfect circle, autonomous and self-contained, emblem and evidence of its own values, immortalizing the ephemeral vision and so offering the gift of life to its readers. (1980)

For Shelley, as for so many other Romantic poets, poetry expanded life, it renewed and replenished life. In *A Defence of Poetry* Shelley wrote: '[p]oetry enlarges the circumference of the imagination by replenishing it with thoughts of ever new delight, which have the power of attracting and assimilating to their own nature all other thoughts, and which form new intervals and interstices whose void forever craves fresh food' (*Selected Poetry and Prose*, 212). For Shelley, as for Keats, Coleridge, Wordsworth and other Romantic poets, the poet is something of a shaman, a magician who conjure up astonishing experiences. As Shelley said in the extract quoted above from *A Defence of Poetry*, '[p]oetry lifts the veil from the hidden beauty of the world and makes familiar objects be as if they were not familiar...' For Shelley, poetry enlarged experience of the world, so that things come alive. For him, poets are shamans, not prophets, but magicians. 'A poet participates in the eternal, the infinite, and the one' said Shelley (*Selected Poetry and Prose*, 207). Shelley's poet creates also for companionship, singing like a nightingale in darkness. 'A poet is a nightingale, who sits in darkness and sings to cheer its own solitude with sweet sounds' (ib., 211). Shelley's huge outpourings, like Coleridge's or Wordsworth's, can be seen as a mirror, a vast form of companionship.

I have chosen representative extracts from the chief poets of the Romantic era in Britain. Due to space, I have been obliged to omit some of the longer poems. I have included some women Romantic poets, not for 'politically correct' reasons (to counter, for example, the way Romantic poetry is seen as a mainly masculine pursuit), but because the women poets produced work as valuable as the male poets.

NOTES

1. W. Jackson Bate: "Keats's Style: Evolution toward Qualities of Permanent Value", in Clarence D. Thorpe *et al*, eds: *The Major English Romantic Poets: A Symposium in Reappraisal*, Southern Illinois University Press 1957.

2. Coleridge: *Collected Letters*, 14 January 1803, II, 916.

3. Peter Redgrove: *The Black Goddess and the Sixth Sense*, Bloomsbury, 1987, 87.

BIBLIOGRAPHY

M.H. Abrams, ed: *English Romantic Poets: Modern Essays in Criticism*, Oxford University Press, New York 1975

W. Jackson Bate: *John Keats*, Chatto & Windus 1979

Catherine Belsey: *Critical Practice*, Routledge 1980

Robert Gittings: *John Keats*, Heinemann 1968

John Keats: *Poems*, ed J.E. Morpurgo, Penguin 1953

—*The Letters of John Keats*, ed Hyder Rollins, 2 vols 1958

Percy Bysshe Shelley: *Selected Poetry and Prose*, Norton, New York, 1977

—*Poetic Works*, ed. Thomas Hutchinson, Oxford University Press, 1905/43

Helen Vendler: *The Odes of John Keats*, Harvard University Press, Cambridge, Mass., 1983

Ailen Ward: *John Keats: The Making of a Poet*, Secker & War-burg 1963

Beauties, Beasts, and Enchantment

CLASSIC FRENCH FAIRY TALES

Translated and with an Introduction
by Jack Zipes

A collection of 36 classic French fairy tales translated by renowned writer Jack Zipes.
Cinderella, Beauty and the Beast, Sleeping Beauty and *Little Red Riding Hood* are among the
classic fairy tales in this amazing book.
Includes illustrations from fairy tale collections.
Jack Zipes has written and published widely on fairy tales.

'Terrific... a succulent array of 17th and 18th century 'salon' fairy tales'
- *The New York Times Book Review*

'These tales are adventurous, thrilling in a way fairy tales are meant to be... The translation
from the French is modern, happily free of archaic and hyperbolic language... a fine and
sophisticated collection' - *New York Tribune*

'Enjoyable to read... a unique collection of French regional folklore' - *Library Journal*

'Charming stories accompanied by attractive pen-and-ink drawings' - *Chattanooga Times*

Introduction and illustrations   612pp.   ISBN 9781861712510 Pbk   ISBN 9781861713193 Hbk

Life, Life
Selected Poems

Arseny Tarkovsky

translated and edited by Virginia Rounding

Arseny Tarkovsky is the neglected Russian poet, father of the acclaimed film director Andrei Tarkovsky. This new book gathers together many of Tarkovsky's most lyrical and heartfelt poems, in Rounding's clear, new translations. Many of Tarkovsky's poems appeared in his son's films, such as *Mirror, Stalker, Nostalghia and The Sacrifice*. There is an introduction by Rounding, and a bibliography of both Arseny and Andrei Tarkovsky.

Bibliography and notes   124pp   3rd ed   ISBN 9781861712660 Hbk   ISBN 9781861711144

MAURICE SENDAK

& the art of children's book illustration

L.M. Poole

Maurice Sendak is the widely acclaimed American children's book author and illustrator. This critical study focuses on his famous trilogy, *Where the Wild Things Are*, *In the Night Kitchen* and *Outside Over There*, as well as the early works and Sendak's superb depictions of the Grimm Brothers' fairy tales in *The Juniper Tree*. L.M. Poole begins with a chapter on children's book illustration, in particular the treatment of fairy tales. Sendak's work is situated within the history of children's book illustration, and he is compared with many contemporary authors.

Fully illustrated. The book has been revised and updated for this edition.

ISBN 9781861714282 Pbk   ISBN 9781861713469 Hbk

In the Dim Void

Samuel Beckett's Late Trilogy:
Company, Ill Seen, Ill Said and Worstward Ho

by Gregory Johns

This book discusses the luminous beauty and dense, rigorous poetry of Samuel Beckett's late works, *Company, Ill Seen, Ill Said* and *Worstward Ho*. Gregory Johns looks back over Beckett's long writing career, charting the development from the *Molloy-Malone Dies-Unnamable* trilogy through the 'fizzles' of the 1960s to the elegiac lyricism of the *Company* series. Johns compares the trilogy with late plays such as *Ghosts, Footfalls* and *Rockaby*.

Bibliography, notes. Illustrated. 120pp
ISBN 9781861712974 Pbk and ISBN 9781861712608 Hbk
9781861713407 E-book

CRESCENT MOON PUBLISHING

web: www.crmoon.com e-mail: cresmopub@yahoo.co.uk

ARTS, PAINTING, SCULPTURE

The Art of Andy Goldsworthy
Andy Goldsworthy: Touching Nature
Andy Goldsworthy in Close-Up
Andy Goldsworthy: Pocket Guide
Andy Goldsworthy In America
Land Art: A Complete Guide
The Art of Richard Long
Richard Long: Pocket Guide
Land Art In the UK
Land Art in Close-Up
Land Art In the U.S.A.
Land Art: Pocket Guide
Installation Art in Close-Up
Minimal Art and Artists In the 1960s and After
Colourfield Painting
Land Art DVD, TV documentary
Andy Goldsworthy DVD, TV documentary
The Erotic Object: Sexuality in Sculpture From Prehistory to the Present Day
Sex in Art: Pornography and Pleasure in Painting and Sculpture
Postwar Art
Sacred Gardens: The Garden in Myth, Religion and Art
Glorification: Religious Abstraction in Renaissance and 20th Century Art
Early Netherlandish Painting
Leonardo da Vinci
Piero della Francesca
Giovanni Bellini
Fra Angelico: Art and Religion in the Renaissance
Mark Rothko: The Art of Transcendence
Frank Stella: American Abstract Artist
Jasper Johns
Brice Marden
Alison Wilding: The Embrace of Sculpture
Vincent van Gogh: Visionary Landscapes
Eric Gill: Nuptials of God
Constantin Brancusi: Sculpting the Essence of Things
Max Beckmann
Caravaggio
Gustave Moreau
Egon Schiele: Sex and Death In Purple Stockings
Delizioso Fotografico Fervore: Works In Process 1
Sacro Cuore: Works In Process 2
The Light Eternal: J.M.W. Turner
The Madonna Glorified: Karen Arthurs

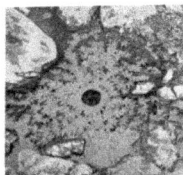

LITERATURE

J.R.R. Tolkien: The Books, The Films, The Whole Cultural Phenomenon
J.R.R. Tolkien: Pocket Guide
Tolkien's Heroic Quest
The *Earthsea* Books of Ursula Le Guin
Beauties, Beasts and Enchantment: Classic French Fairy Tales
German Popular Stories by the Brothers Grimm
Philip Pullman and *His Dark Materials*
Sexing Hardy: Thomas Hardy and Feminism
Thomas Hardy's *Tess of the d'Urbervilles*
Thomas Hardy's *Jude the Obscure*
Thomas Hardy: The Tragic Novels
Love and Tragedy: Thomas Hardy
The Poetry of Landscape in Hardy
Wessex Revisited: Thomas Hardy and John Cowper Powys
Wolfgang Iser: Essays and Interviews
Petrarch, Dante and the Troubadours
Maurice Sendak and the Art of Children's Book Illustration
Andrea Dworkin
Cixous, Irigaray, Kristeva: The *Jouissance* of French Feminism
Julia Kristeva: Art, Love, Melancholy, Philosophy, Semiotics and Psychoanalysis
Hélene Cixous I Love You: The *Jouissance* of Writing
Luce Irigaray: Lips, Kissing, and the Politics of Sexual Difference
Peter Redgrove: Here Comes the Flood
Peter Redgrove: Sex-Magic-Poetry-Cornwall
Lawrence Durrell: Between Love and Death, East and West
Love, Culture & Poetry: Lawrence Durrell
Cavafy: Anatomy of a Soul
German Romantic Poetry: Goethe, Novalis, Heine, Hölderlin
Feminism and Shakespeare
Shakespeare: Love, Poetry & Magic
The Passion of D.H. Lawrence
D.H. Lawrence: Symbolic Landscapes
D.H. Lawrence: Infinite Sensual Violence
Rimbaud: Arthur Rimbaud and the Magic of Poetry
The Ecstasies of John Cowper Powys
Sensualism and Mythology: The Wessex Novels of John Cowper Powys
Amorous Life: John Cowper Powys and the Manifestation of Affectivity (H.W. Fawkner)
Postmodern Powys: New Essays on John Cowper Powys (Joe Boulter)
Rethinking Powys: Critical Essays on John Cowper Powys
Paul Bowles & Bernardo Bertolucci
Rainer Maria Rilke
Joseph Conrad: *Heart of Darkness*
In the Dim Void: Samuel Beckett
Samuel Beckett Goes into the Silence
André Gide: Fiction and Fervour
Jackie Collins and the Blockbuster Novel
Blinded By Her Light: The Love-Poetry of Robert Graves
The Passion of Colours: Travels In Mediterranean Lands
Poetic Forms

POETRY

Ursula Le Guin: Walking In Cornwall
Peter Redgrove: Here Comes The Flood
Peter Redgrove: Sex-Magic-Poetry-Cornwall
Dante: Selections From the Vita Nuova
Petrarch, Dante and the Troubadours
William Shakespeare: Sonnets
William Shakespeare: Complete Poems
Blinded By Her Light: The Love-Poetry of Robert Graves
Emily Dickinson: Selected Poems
Emily Brontë: Poems
Thomas Hardy: Selected Poems
Percy Bysshe Shelley: Poems
John Keats: Selected Poems
Joh n Keats: Poems of 1820
D.H. Lawrence: Selected Poems
Edmund Spenser: Poems
Edmund Spenser: Amoretti
John Donne: Poems
Henry Vaughan: Poems
Sir Thomas Wyatt: Poems
Robert Herrick: Selected Poems
Rilke: Space, Essence and Angels in the Poetry of Rainer Maria Rilke
Rainer Maria Rilke: Selected Poems
Friedrich Hölderlin: Selected Poems
Arseny Tarkovsky: Selected Poems
Arthur Rimbaud: Selected Poems
Arthur Rimbaud: A Season in Hell
Arthur Rimbaud and the Magic of Poetry
Novalis: Hymns To the Night
German Romantic Poetry
Paul Verlaine: Selected Poems
Elizaethan Sonnet Cycles
D.J. Enright: By-Blows
Jeremy Reed: Brigitte's Blue Heart
Jeremy Reed: Claudia Schiffer's Red Shoes
Gorgeous Little Orpheus
Radiance: New Poems
Crescent Moon Book of Nature Poetry
Crescent Moon Book of Love Poetry
Crescent Moon Book of Mystical Poetry
Crescent Moon Book of Elizabethan Love Poetry
Crescent Moon Book of Metaphysical Poetry
Crescent Moon Book of Romantic Poetry
Pagan America: New American Poetry

MEDIA, CINEMA, FEMINISM and CULTURAL STUDIES

J.R.R. Tolkien: The Books, The Films, The Whole Cultural Phenomenon
J.R.R. Tolkien: Pocket Guide
The *Lord of the Rings* Movies: Pocket Guide
The Cinema of Hayao Miyazaki
Hayao Miyazaki: *Princess Mononoke*: Pocket Movie Guide
Hayao Miyazaki: *Spirited Away*: Pocket Movie Guide
Tim Burton : Hallowe'en For Hollywood
Ken Russell
Ken Russell: *Tommy*: Pocket Movie Guide
The Ghost Dance: The Origins of Religion
The Peyote Cult
Cixous, Irigaray, Kristeva: The *Jouissance* of French Feminism
Julia Kristeva: Art, Love, Melancholy, Philosophy, Semiotics and Psychoanalysis
Luce Irigaray: Lips, Kissing, and the Politics of Sexual Difference
Hélene Cixous I Love You: The *Jouissance* of Writing
Andrea Dworkin
'Cosmo Woman': The World of Women's Magazines
Women in Pop Music
HomeGround: The Kate Bush Anthology
Discovering the Goddess (Geoffrey Ashe)
The Poetry of Cinema
The Sacred Cinema of Andrei Tarkovsky
Andrei Tarkovsky: Pocket Guide
Andrei Tarkovsky: *Mirror*: Pocket Movie Guide
Andrei Tarkovsky: *The Sacrifice*: Pocket Movie Guide
Walerian Borowczyk: Cinema of Erotic Dreams
Jean-Luc Godard: The Passion of Cinema
Jean-Luc Godard: *Hail Mary*: Pocket Movie Guide
Jean-Luc Godard: *Contempt*: Pocket Movie Guide
Jean-Luc Godard: *Pierrot le Fou*: Pocket Movie Guide
John Hughes and Eighties Cinema
Ferris Bueller's Day Off: Pocket Movie Guide
Jean-Luc Godard: Pocket Guide
The Cinema of Richard Linklater
Liv Tyler: Star In Ascendance
Blade Runner and the Films of Philip K. Dick
Paul Bowles and Bernardo Bertolucci
Media Hell: Radio, TV and the Press
An Open Letter to the BBC
Detonation Britain: Nuclear War in the UK
Feminism and Shakespeare
Wild Zones: Pornography, Art and Feminism
Sex in Art: Pornography and Pleasure in Painting and Sculpture
Sexing Hardy: Thomas Hardy and Feminism

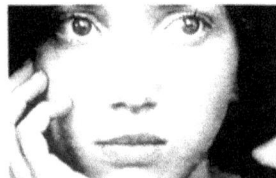

The Light Eternal is a model monograph, an exemplary job. The subject matter of the book is beautifully
organised and dead on beam. (Lawrence Durrell)
It is amazing for me to see my work treated with such passion and respect. (Andrea Dworkin)

CRESCENT MOON PUBLISHING
P.O. Box 1312, Maidstone, Kent, ME14 5XU, Great Britain. www.crmoon.com

cresmopub@yahoo.co.uk   www.crescentmoon.org.uk